WARRIOR WOMAN

BOOT CAMP

KELLY HAWKINS

LifeCare
·Publishing

LifeCare Publishing is a branch of
LifeCare Christian Center
A non-profit faith-based ministry
www.LifeCareChristianCenter.org
info.lifecarecc@gmail.com
Westland, MI USA

Mission Statement

LifeCare Christian Center exists to partner with individuals, churches
and the community in promoting spiritual, emotional, physical and
relational wholeness by providing quality, affordable care, education
and training services from a Christian perspective.

For
Cheryl Weeks-Rosten
Renee Allen
Marilyn Osborne
Candi Beemer

Although you probably wouldn't see yourself this way,
each of you, in my youth, was a warrior who fought for me.
Whether it was as a teacher, a coach, a family friend who
watched over me, a mentor, or some of each, each of you spoke
words of life and displayed acts of love that battled and defeated
darkness within me, giving me life and purpose.
I'm grateful that you showed up for the battle!

Lord, would You thread throughout these pages the same
powerful love that I've experienced from each of these women,
that those reading would have Your love sewn into their hearts in
new and beautiful ways.

CONTENTS

FOREWORD

At the end of 2019, four gals (Stephanie, Belynda, Wanda and I) began praying and brainstorming about a Bible Study in our senior living community. Along the way we consulted with a pastor (Gayle) and added two more neighbors (Eleanor and Wanda) to establish the core for the beginning class. We had several gatherings in the community clubhouse when Covid hit, and we had to learn to Zoom. At the end of 2020 we were together, masked and in the clubhouse, studying **The Armor of God** by Priscilla Shirer (Lifeway Publishing). Little did I know that would be the last study I would complete in my Charlotte community. My soulmate of almost 55 years, Larry, chose to stop all meds and procedures that he had endured for almost 25 years. We rented an apartment closer to our son Ken's family to use as an opened door hospice (for one month Larry was **Waiting For Heaven** and he arrived there on February 28, 2021). Six months after Larry's passing I met Kelly, before the turmoil of selling our Charlotte home, changing addresses three times and settling into a new home.

In March of 2022 I saw Kelly again, and shortly after that second meeting Kelly asked if I would write a foreword for her latest book, **Warrior Woman: Boot Camp**. Little did she know that in the months since Larry passed, I was too weary and exhausted to put on the Armor of God. As I read Kelly's book, I started putting on that armor (Ephesians 6), a good reminder of the last Bible study I had done in my former neighborhood. When reading **Warrior Woman**, I underlined things I wanted to review, and I did the action points at the end of the chapters. I also got a renewed desire to go over the journey Larry and I had traveled, sort of a good rearview look in the mirror to remember that I was a Warrior Woman and I was still here for battle. Kelly triggered bittersweet tears in my eyes, not what she wrote but the way I processed a verse or thought that she mentioned. For example, she gave us part of the Warrior Woman plan in I Peter 5:8-9, "Be sober, be vigilant because your adversary the devil, as a roaring lion, walketh about seeking whom he may devour." Every morning Larry and I prayed the same prayer together for decades. When away from each other we'd say it over the phone, sometimes just leaving our part on voicemail. My part was from I Peter 5:9, "Father, help us to recognize and stand against the evil one today" (a memory lane moment). I no longer had a partner to pray his part, but I was inspired by reading **Warrior Woman** to pray my part. I finally started to communicate with God after months of exhaustion and trudging through what felt like wet cement. Another reference came from a book Larry authored, **The Papa Prayer**, "Nothing changes the human heart so deeply as to look bad in the presence of love." Still seeing his name and words in print makes my heart skip a beat and miss him, but it leads me to take what he has written and apply it to myself, just like he's talking to me.

Often Kelly's writing style reminded me of pillows with embroidered sayings on them. Every once in a while you find a phrase or a verse in her book that needs to be copied somewhere. I want to share a few of the pillows/tee shirts (as a collector of tee shirt sayings) she painted in my mind:

- Carry a saber, not a glow stick
- Accept your own inability and remember God's ability

- There is purpose in a pause
- Be careful not to fight as if the battle belongs to you
- Make God look good

Read and enjoy Kelly's challenging work, **Warrior Woman: Boot Camp.** I have and I can recommend this book for the way it strengthened me to pick up the belt of truth, the breastplate of righteousness, the shoes of peace, the shield of faith, the helmet of salvation, and the sword of the Spirit all wrapped up in prayer. In the introduction Kelly mentioned "I have a God who is sovereign over timing and able to hold my armor in place even when I don't feel ready." I also have to remember that I'm in a battle not against flesh and blood, but against the powers of this dark world and against the spiritual forces of evil in the heavenly realms.

Put on the whole armor of God. Ephesians 6

The Lord is with you mighty warrior. Judges 6:12

Your righteousness shall go before you; the glory of the Lord shall be your rearguard. Isaiah 58:8 (We think of armor covering only the front, but when we go into battle with God we must not forget that He has our back.)

I look forward to getting to know Kelly even more in the years to come.

Rachael Crabb

PREFACE

Boot Camp. A military website describes it this way:

Basic Training — often called boot camp — prepares recruits for all elements of service: physical, mental and emotional. It gives service members the basic tools necessary to perform the roles that will be assigned to them for the duration of their tour. (Todaysmilitary.com)

Many of us will have, on average, about 70-80 years as "service members" in this life. Boot Camp for a follower of Christ never really comes to an end; we keep growing and being prepared for deeper and deeper connection with Christ and others. Our faith continues to be stretched. Physically, mentally, emotionally and spiritually, we continue to be challenged throughout our lives. In many ways, we continue to grow stronger, until we grow weaker. I believe it's when we eventually grow weaker (or actually embrace our weakness) that we're finally able to see our greatest strength. My hope is that this book will give you Boot Camp tools to further equip you as you align even more closely with Christ for the duration of your "tour" in this life. Our time is short. Train well.

TRAINING

"So put on all the armor that God gives. Then
when the evil day comes, you will be able to
defend yourself. And when the battle is over,
you will still be standing firm."
–Ephesians 6.13, ESV

I was training for battle as the morning light poured in my window. Every word I read and studied further equipped me with a strong, sharp sword. I shared my heart with the Lord, and I poured out my cares and concerns to Him. God prepared my feet to walk in peace as I filled my thoughts with His words. I asked Him to give me a mind to discern truth, knowing that truth would hold my armor in place. I recognized my tendency to pursue things apart from God. So I asked Him to help me pursue righteousness in order to protect my heart. I resolved to reserve my whole heart for Him.

Questions and anxieties began to fill my mind. I chose to trust God whatever happened, confident that He would be sovereign over everything. I told Him that I would believe. I asked Him to help me in the places where I fell short in believing. I knew this was the only way I could defeat the attacks of the enemy.

God reminded me that "whoever calls upon the name of the Lord will be saved" (Romans 10.13), and that every time I call on Him, He will protect my mind, as well as the authority that He gives me.

With the light that began to pour in my window, there also came movement into the day. That movement brought opportunities to apply my preparation for warfare, although sooner than I had hoped. My armor was needed even before it was fully secured in place.

A startling knock on my door grabbed my attention. My son dragged himself heavily into my room, collapsing on the floor. His stabbing headache pulled me to his side as he lay there, writhing in pain. My attention focused on him, caring for his needs. Fortunately, I have a God who is sovereign over timing and able to hold my armor in place even when I don't feel ready.

The training ground for battle never feels complete, and I never feel fully ready. Still, I step into the moments that seem to run after me as if they're attacking me. God promises to go with me, and He's the one giving my arms strength to fight the battle. Whatever is needed as I step into the battles of life, God is right there in it with me, fully ready.

I haven't started every day with equipping like this. These last couple years, we've been trudging through a worldwide crisis. We've all had to learn how to navigate life in a new way. For the first few months, like everyone else, my world was turned upside down. My schedule was completely thrown off, ministry as we knew it came to a halt, and I was unusually surrounded by my household. My time with the Lord was sporadic, and my armor was left scattered through the pages of my Bible and draped over my quiet time chair like yesterday's clothes.

Different seasons can do that to us—throw us into a tailspin until we regain our bearings and grab onto those pieces of armor once again. We have to choose it one day at a time. Each of those days, God is waiting for us—to help us strap on each piece of the armor. In those times, it's refreshing to be equipped, but what's even more refreshing is intimately connecting with the One who equips us.

I may not always be ready for the battle, but because my God is always ready, I'm a warrior woman who is equipped, empowered and enjoyed.

As you read through this book, grab a pen and underline what stands out to you so you can easily go back to it. Take notes in the margin of what it means to you personally. Also, use a journal to write down key phrases that stand out to you and the impact they have on you.

2 Corinthians 10.3-5

HOW WE WAGE WAR

3For though we live in the world, we do not wage war as the world does. 4The weapons we fight with are not the weapons of the world. On the contrary, they have divine power to demolish strongholds. 5We demolish arguments and every pretension that sets itself up against the knowledge of God, and we take captive every thought to make it obedient to Christ.

Ephesians 6.10-18

THE ARMOR OF GOD

[10]*Finally, be strong in the Lord and in his mighty power.* [11]*Put on the full armor of God, so that you can take your stand against the devil's schemes.* [12]*For our struggle is not against flesh and blood, but against the rulers, against the authorities, against the powers of this dark world and against the spiritual forces of evil in the heavenly realms.* [13]*Therefore put on the full armor of God, so that when the day of evil comes, you may be able to stand your ground, and after you have done everything, to stand.* [14]*Stand firm then, with the belt of truth buckled around your waist, with the breastplate of righteousness in place,* [15]*and with your feet fitted with the readiness that comes from the gospel of peace.* [16]*In addition to all this, take up the shield of faith, with which you can extinguish all the flaming arrows of the evil one.* [17]*Take the helmet of salvation and the sword of the Spirit, which is the word of God.*

[18]*And pray in the Spirit on all occasions with all kinds of prayers and requests. With this in mind, be alert and always keep on praying for all the Lord's people.*

WHY A WARRIOR BATTLES

1

SHADOWS & LIGHT SABERS

"I will make you a light." –Isaiah 49.6, NLT

My eyes weren't even open yet. It was that moment of partial awareness as I was awakening from a deep sleep. Suddenly, my brain spun out at full speed with this headline question: "WHY DO I HAVE TO BE A LIGHT BEARER?!?"

With my eyes still closed, I saw myself holding what appeared as a light saber from Star Wars. My immediate response to my own question was, "It's easier just to stay in the shadows."

It's true. It usually is easier in many ways to stay in the shadows. I've spent most of my life in the shadows—avoiding the spotlight and not making waves. Although I was in the shadows, I certainly wasn't about darkness. I believed in the light. I believed in *being* a light. I just chose to carry more of a dim glow stick that wouldn't attract attention rather than a torch or a light saber that drew everyone's attention— especially the enemy's. My goal was to stay under his radar.

Certainly understandable—enemies are scary. I guess my goal was to stay under most people's radar. It felt safer that way.

But the shadows caused some trouble for me. God didn't intend for me to live in the shadows, and when I've lived apart from God's intention for me, I've found something dying in my soul. In those times, my heart reflected the same dimness as my glow stick until I came to my breaking point. I couldn't live this way anymore—I wasn't living out all that God had called me to be, and I felt like I was dying.

That's when I found my voice, my convictions and my determination—and a light saber that replaced my glow stick. Ultimately, I began to truly live. But it certainly hasn't been an easy path. Being a light bearer carrying a light saber has put me in the position of needing to speak truth in love when silence would be much less disruptive. It's caused me to draw others out and try to listen with compassion and understanding when a defensive silent-treatment was preferred. It's required me to take responsibility for my choices rather than defer to someone else. It's motivated me to reach out and care for or defend others when quietly going about my own business would have been more comfortable. It's challenged me to pour myself out and face giants when doing nothing would have been less costly.

I have learned the value in living as a light bearer, and I wouldn't want to go back to living any other way. Still, there are moments when I just get tired of the battle to bear light. I hear the tempting voices that try to draw me back into the shadows. But I clearly know that I never want to go back to living in the shadows—for me it was the valley of the shadow of death that God has brought me through and out of. Now I get to live as a bearer of light and life—a privilege the God of all creation has given me. So I will carry my light—the saber, not the glow stick—with honor.

Since you've picked up this book, I imagine you might be inclined to do the same, and that thought of being light bearers together brings me joy.

CAPTIVES SET FREE

I have experienced others running into the darkness to free me. The thing about living in dark shadows is that you often don't know anything else. You don't know how it's supposed to be different until someone runs in, grabs your hand and leads you out into the light.

God intends for us to live in the light of truth. He says that's what will set us free. (John 8.32) It's for freedom that He sets us free. (Galatians 5.1 and Luke 4.18) But this life has a way of casting shadows on God's truth.

We all have various experiences throughout our lives that cause us to draw conclusions about ourselves. Those conclusions embed themselves in our hearts and become beliefs that steer our lives. Those beliefs are sometimes true—providing light, freedom and often a sense of peace. Other times, they are false—covering us with dark shadows, bondage and often a sense of negative emotion.

When I entered high school, two older girls began bullying me on the school bus. Almost daily, they threatened to beat me up. Fortunately, I took the news to my dad who, supportively, spoke truth to me. He reminded me of my value and strength. He told me to never throw the first punch, but if they do, he would support me in defending myself. Because of that, I knew they were wrong in the things they said to me, and I knew I had a defender on my side affirming who I was. Maybe it was because of renewed confidence and the way I carried myself after that discussion with my dad, but I never did have to defend myself, and as far as I can remember, those girls never bothered me after that.

With other experiences, I drew my own conclusions and developed beliefs that I wrongly thought were truth. Those beliefs held me in deceptive shadows of bondage for years. As a young girl, I was a loner and didn't have great social skills, but I wanted to be accepted. One of the beliefs I developed was that I needed approval from others to be acceptable. That belief led me to be a chameleon in my relationships. I tried to adapt myself to what others were like. The things they liked became the things I liked. Their mannerisms became my mannerisms. I figured if I was like them, then they would like me, and I would therefore have approval and acceptance. I didn't consciously think about this, it just naturally derived from my belief. Ultimately, it led to a lot of disappointment and heartache, even into my late thirties, to the point that I felt like I was dying inside. I had no freedom to just be me.

Beliefs like this prevented me from loving God and loving others as He intended. Fortunately, I learned that real change was possible. Those deceptive shadows can be exposed so that we can hear God's truth in our beliefs. Once I began to hear God's truth in my specific beliefs, transformation began to happen in my thoughts and actions. I saw the reality of what Paul meant when he said to "be transformed by the renewing of your mind." (Romans 12.2) As a result, I had a new perspective on life. Peace began to overtake heaviness and control, and joy began to show up without effort. I didn't have to make life work like I thought I had to before.

I know what it's like when a captive is set free. One reason I'm passionate about being a warrior woman is that I see hope for people. I want to shine light that will set captives free!

WHO A WARRIOR IS

2

GIDEON: THE WEAKEST ON THE LOSING TEAM

"The Lord turned to him and said,
'Go in the strength you have....'"
–Judges 6.14a

I n the Star Wars movies, you see warriors who are passionate about their mission. At some point, a weakness is revealed in each one of them. Sometimes you see the good guys return to their master, Yoda. He's a good master who seeks to empower them and help them stay connected to their greatest strength.

In the Hunger Games movies, Cinna does not just design clothes for Katniss, but he encourages and empowers her. He gives her confidence and reminds her of what she has to offer as a warrior.

Every good warrior needs someone who believes in her and draws out her strength. In the Bible, Gideon was aware of his weakness, but God knew he had strength beyond the weakness where Gideon focused. Although Gideon's eyes were on his weakness, God drew his attention to the strength that He had instilled in Gideon.

Because the Israelites did evil in the eyes of the Lord, God withheld His protection from them as many groups of eastern peoples oppressed them and invaded and ravaged their land, their crops and their livestock for seven years. The Israelites feared for their lives and hid in caves and mountain clefts.

> [7]When the Israelites cried out to the Lord because of Midian, [8]he sent them a prophet, who said, "This is what the Lord, the God of Israel, says: I brought you up out of Egypt, out of the land of slavery. [9]I rescued you from the hand of the Egyptians. And I delivered you from the hand of all your oppressors; I drove them out before you and gave you their land. [10]I said to you, 'I am the Lord your God; do not worship the gods of the Amorites, in whose land you live.' But you have not listened to me." (Judges 6.7-10)

The stage is set. The losing team cries out to God for help. Then the angel of the Lord comes and sits by Gideon and chats with him. Gideon shrinks back in fear. He is, after all, on the losing team. His own words focus on his weakness, describing himself as being from "the weakest clan" and "the least" in his family. But the angel of the Lord speaks truth to the fear that binds Gideon: "'The Lord is with you, mighty warrior.'" (Judges 6.12)

Gideon certainly heard the beginning of that statement, and I love his respectful question, clearly aware that his people haven't seen much good in a very long time:

"Pardon me, my lord," Gideon replied, "but if the Lord is with us, why has all this happened to us? Where are all his wonders that our ancestors told us about when they said, 'Did not the Lord bring us up out of Egypt?' But now the Lord has abandoned us and given us into the hand of Midian." (Judges 6.13)

The Lord doesn't answer his questions. He redirects him, empowering him and instilling confidence in him by highlighting his strength once again: "The Lord turned to him and said, 'Go in the strength you have and save Israel out of Midian's hand. Am I not sending you?'" (Judges 6.14)

With a very polite question, we clearly see how Gideon sees himself: "'Pardon me, my lord,' Gideon replied, 'but how can I save Israel? My clan is the weakest in Manasseh, and I am the least in my family.'" (Judges 6.15)

We already know that the Lord called him a mighty warrior, something no one else would have called him. The Lord wanted him to see himself as *He* saw him, and to go out as a mighty warrior, completely dependent on God's saving power.

"The Lord answered, 'I will be with you....'" (Judges 6.16)

When we go out, filled with all the weakness that has always plagued us, our calling is to align with God in the battle He has for us, and then rely on His direction and power to succeed.

It was not Gideon's weakness (or strength) that made him a mighty warrior. Both weak people and strong people can be warriors. What I see in Gideon is that he knew and accepted his own inability. However, he also knew God's ability. Since nothing is hidden from God, God himself knew all the strengths and weaknesses of Gideon (after all, he was designed by God). God knew that His own power could be displayed through Gideon. God also knew Gideon would cooperate with putting God's power on display.

For any successful warrior for Christ, we must know that we can only be a mighty warrior if God's power is what's on display, not ours. When we trust in God's provision, we go in the strength that God gives. And we go with the faith that God will provide whatever is needed to accomplish what He wants to accomplish.

What is God calling you to, "mighty warrior"?
Take some time to journal what the Lord brings to mind.

"SO WHEN I FIGHT,
I'LL FIGHT ON MY KNEES
WITH MY HANDS LIFTED
HIGH. OH GOD, THE
BATTLE BELONGS TO YOU."
"Battle Belongs" -Phil Wickham

3

ESTHER: LIVING BEYOND CONTROL

"Let perseverance finish its work so that you
may be mature and complete, not lacking
anything." –James 1.4

Sometimes we wish things were different. Maybe it's grieving the loss of a loved one. Maybe it's losing control of something that's important to us. Maybe it's struggling with unfilled hopes in a marriage or simply wishing you were married. Maybe it's anguish over circumstances with a child, or lamenting that an illness has stolen our time, energy, freedom and finances. Or maybe just that every time we get a vacation or a break, when we come back, we end up with more work.

It's hard when control is taken from us. It's hard when what was comfortable to us is suddenly exchanged for something less comfortable. It's devastating when our hopes are crushed. Turning our hope toward God's loving hand is ultimately where our peace will be found, but grieving our losses is crucial.

This was Esther's experience, just as it is ours. Esther (a.k.a. Hadassah) was a Jewish girl who understood grief and loss. She was orphaned and then raised by her cousin, Mordecai, until she was probably around 15 years old. At that time, the middle-aged king (Xerxes) ordered that many young, beautiful women be brought into his harem because he was looking for a new, young wife. Esther was put under the charge of Hegai, the king's eunuch who was responsible for all of the king's harem. Esther won his favor and was given special treatment. She continued to find favor with everyone in the palace and ultimately found favor with the king. The king then chose Esther to be his wife. Throughout all of this, "Esther had not revealed her nationality and family background, because Mordecai had forbidden her to do so." (Esther 2.10)

As much as he could do so outside of the palace, Mordecai continued to check on Esther. "Every day he walked back and forth near the courtyard of the harem to find out how Esther was and what was happening to her." (Esther 2.11)

About five years passed. One of the king's most highly regarded nobles, Haman, developed a plot to destroy the Jews. Haman deceptively garnered the king's full support. His plot would eradicate Esther's entire childhood community, where she was still secretly connected and counseled by her caring cousin. As Esther had done her whole life, she listened to her cousin Mordecai's wise direction as he urged her to risk her life to go to talk to the king. This was an unacceptable practice that could result in her death. A king could be approached only by invitation. Still, Mordecai called Esther to be a warrior and go before the king: "'For if you remain silent at this time, relief and deliverance for the Jews will arise from another place, but you and your father's family will perish.

And who knows but that you have come to your royal position for such a time as this?'" (Esther 4.14)

Esther had been through so much already. So much control had been taken from her through her whole young life, and yet she understood her cousin's words—that she may have gone through all this just to have this opportunity to preserve the Jewish nation. Her choice was to step up and be the warrior in the circumstances where God put her. She responded to Mordecai:

> [16]"Go, gather together all the Jews who are in Susa, and fast for me. Do not eat or drink for three days, night or day. I and my attendants will fast as you do. When this is done, I will go to the king, even though it is against the law. And if I perish, I perish."
> [17]So Mordecai went away and carried out all of Esther's instructions. (Esther 4.16-17)

All that you have gone through might also be for a very significant purpose. I always wonder about this when I'm facing difficulties, grieving a loss or losing some sort of control.

As I try to hold my hands open to God's plans, knowing He causes all things to work together for good for those who follow Him (Romans 8.28), some questions I ponder in these times are:

- *What do You (God) want to do in this situation?*
- *What part would You like me to play in this?*
- *How can I honor You and help fulfill Your good plans?*

God has already gone before us and knows everything we will walk into—everything we will face, and He says about it, "'For I know the plans I have for you,' says the Lord. 'They are plans for good and not for disaster, to give you a future and a hope.'" (Jeremiah 29.11, NLT) Certainly, not everything we face is good in itself, but when we entrust it to God's hands, He makes even the bad things work out for good.

When we face any loss, it's important for us to grieve that loss, to feel the sadness and all the other emotions that accompany it. At the right time, we will be able to release our grip on and affectionately hold the memory of what we had and what we had hoped for the future. In time, we will embrace a new future wrapped in God's arms.

We've gone through two years of the COVID-19 crisis, and my friend Krystina was married right at the beginning of the crisis. It squelched many of her hopes for her first year of marriage, and as she processed her feelings, she wrote this:

> If you look for hope the way you think it should be packaged up, you might just miss it. You will miss the moments that we often take for granted. You will mistake a disappointment for an opportunity. You will mistake heartache for healing in places you never knew you needed. Look for hope, but know that it doesn't always come the way you expect it to.
>
> "So let it grow, and don't try to squirm out of your problems. For when your patience is finally in full bloom, then you will be ready for anything, strong in character, full and complete." (James 1.4, TLB)
>
> "And let endurance have its full effect, so that you may be mature and complete, lacking nothing." (CSB)

You can't bank on the struggle passing, but you can know this: the struggle can cause you to lack nothing.

One thing I love about Esther is that I don't see her squirming. Do you tend to squirm? I hate to say it, but I do. But I'm getting a new perspective on problems and challenges. James 1.4 tells me that when I endure and let endurance finish what it has to do in me, then I will lack nothing. Wouldn't that be amazing to lack nothing? That motivates me to want to endure what comes my way. It motivates me to finish reading books I start, to finish my intended exercise routine before quitting early, to continue loving that hard-to-love person and to keep trusting God as I move through the uncertainty and pain I face in this life.

What is one thing you are now more motivated to endure?

"A woman of strength knows to take the time to prepare herself…she goes into seclusion for a season if necessary, to gather the strength of God's power to perform what is required." -Neva Coyle

4

JOB: UGLY IN THE PRESENCE OF LOVE

"But because of his great love for us, God,
who is rich in mercy, made us alive with Christ
even when we were dead in transgressions—it
is by grace you have been saved."
–Ephesians 2.4-5

Larry Crabb said, "Nothing changes the human heart so deeply as to look bad in the presence of love, to be seen with all that is wickedly ugly about us and still be wanted, more, to be delighted in. That's grace." (Crabb, *The Papa Prayer*).

I was 18 years old and a freshman in college when I met Candi, who was five years older than I was and newly married. She and her husband had just planted a church on my college campus. I was the first student to get involved. I was a lonely college student looking for purpose and community. She was praying for someone like me to connect with in ministry and life. I was quiet, insecure and self-conscious. She was loving and joyfully passionate about serving the Lord. Her enthusiasm for life and her love for God drew my interest. God connected our lives.

Within just a few weeks of meeting her, I was at her house for a Bible study. My lower back became increasingly achy, and by the end of our Bible study, I was flat on my back on her living room floor. I got up and made it back to my dorm room, but in the middle of the night, I was in so much pain that my roommate, Kathy, took me to the ER. Writhing in pain through the night in the ER, Kathy stayed with me so I wouldn't be alone and to communicate with the doctors and staff. In the late morning, the doctors determined that I had a kidney stone. I was still in tremendous pain as a visitor arrived. By that time, the pain was so extreme that it brought nausea and vomiting, witnessed by Candi as she walked in the room. I felt embarrassed, but Candi was very reassuring and completely loving. I looked ugly in the presence of Candi's love. That was not my choice of how I wanted to present myself to my new friend that morning. However, there's something about looking ugly in the presence of love that creates a beautiful bond. Nearly four decades later, she is still one of my dearest friends. Not only that, I also know that since Candi has already seen me at my worst, I can be completely authentic with her, knowing I will continue to be loved.

Years later, when faced with some identity challenges that felt shameful, I gradually opened up to Lillian. I had gotten to know her a bit and watched how she led her life. I watched her with others as she counseled and guided them toward wholeness. She was always filled with grace and compassion as she loved and served the Lord. It gave me a glimmer of hope that I could be completely open with her about my ugliness. It was scary, so I tested the waters at first, and her responses were refreshing. Lillian listened with compassion and understanding, and then walked with me through a journey of healing the roots of my struggle. Because I could be ugly in the presence of Lillian's love, I can now live freely as the woman God created me to be. I no longer "white-knuckle" it through life, and I don't have to be a chameleon. I can be who God designed me to be. Lillian saw what, to me, felt shameful and ugly, and she provided a presence of love that allowed me to be authentic. Her grace provided a safe space for me to align with God's intent for me. She knew that God's design was IN me; it was just covered by coping strategies and skewed beliefs from wounds that disguised it. Freedom to be ugly in the presence of love deeply changed my heart.

In the Bible, in the book of Job, Job is described as a blameless man with complete integrity. His desire was to honor God, and at the same time, he was committed to being authentic.

Job experienced tremendous losses that included the deaths of all of his ten children, most of his servants, most, if not all, of his animals and terrible boils all over his skin. In addition to all of that, his wife gave up on God. His close friends sat silently mourning with him for seven days, but once they started talking, they heaped more pain on him.

Job tried to talk of his anguish as he wrestled with God over his pain and loss, but his friends talked incessantly about how Job must have done wrong. This went on for a very long time (for 33 chapters in the book!). As my friend Diana says, "God often calls us to long-suffering, but we try to make it short-suffering." Job's friends were uncomfortable with Job's long-suffering and were trying to get him over it (short-suffering).

Finally, after much testing of Job's patience, God responded—after waiting for just the right time. God was willing to allow Job to wrestle with Him, and even look ugly, in His presence of love. God knows that there's much for us to learn in our suffering, and He tends not to rush our learning process. When God finally responded, Job realized that even when he couldn't understand God's ways, he could still trust His heart.

When God replied to Job's friends, He confronted their mistreatment of Job and misrepresentation of Him (Job 42.7). God sees when we are mistreated, and He determines the right time to confront. When confronted at the right time, Job's friends repented and obeyed God. (Job 42.9) Because of how God impacted Job's heart, Job was able to pray for his friends who mistreated him, and God honored Job's obedience. (Job 42.10-11) Those same friends then consoled and comforted Job. God then poured out tremendous blessings on Job—more in the second half of his life than in the first.

I believe that Job's friends finally learned how to let someone look ugly in the presence of love.

What is there that is ugly in you that you've tried to hide?

Will you take a step and seek a safe, loving friend who is aligned with God? Then take baby steps in sharing those things that might be scary to share. When you discover that you can be ugly in the presence of love, it will transform your life in beautiful ways.

"NOTHING CHANGES THE HUMAN HEART SO DEEPLY AS TO LOOK BAD IN THE PRESENCE OF LOVE"

Larry Crabb, The Papa Prayer

HOW A WARRIOR IS

DEVELOPED

5

INFUSED

"He gives strength to the weary and increases
the power of the weak."
–Isaiah 40.29

I believe God can do anything; I just don't believe He can do anything through *ME*.

I enjoy gardening. Sometimes I use a trowel to do jobs that it wasn't intended to do—like pry out roots. I don't even know how many trowels I've broken because they were weaker than the power I used to try to make them accomplish a job they were too weak to do.

I imagine God's hands having the strength of solid iron. Anything He uses His hands for certainly wouldn't break His hands. But I'm weak like the trowel. When I consider God using me, I sometimes see myself as that flimsy trowel in God's strong hand. I would break and be useless to Him.

I believe God can do anything... when He's not limited by my weakness. Too often I still focus on what I can do. The good news is that it just doesn't matter what I'm capable of; He is able to accomplish anything He chooses, even with weak tools—oftentimes, especially with weak tools.

When I lean on His strength for a task He calls me to, His hands of iron strength actually infuse me as the tool to complete every good work that He sets out to accomplish through me. So rather than my strength failing under God's, His strength infuses and envelops mine.

The Apostle Paul learned God's perspective regarding his weakness:

> But he said to me, "My grace is sufficient for you, for my power is made perfect in weakness." Therefore I will boast all the more gladly about my weaknesses, so that Christ's power may rest on me. [10]That is why, for Christ's sake, I delight in weaknesses, in insults, in hardships, in persecutions, in difficulties. For when I am weak, then I am strong. (2 Corinthians 12.9-10)

As warriors, we are infused with God's strength to accomplish every mission He gives us.

Consider an area in your life where God is leading you to serve Him, but you feel too weak. In your journal, describe your feelings, and then ask God for His perspective on it. Write down: "Isaiah 40.29, 'He gives strength to the weary and increases the power of the weak.'" What is God speaking to you about this verse and how it applies to your feelings?

"MY HELP COMES FROM YOU

YOU'RE RIGHT HERE, PULLING ME THROUGH

YOU CARRY MY WEAKNESS, MY SICKNESS, MY BROKENNESS ALL ON YOUR SHOULDERS"

"Shoulders" –For King & Country

6

SEASONS

"Does he not see my ways and count my
every step?" –Job 31.4

You may not remember the first step you took as a baby, in the first season of your life, but what about all the other "first steps" in your life since then? I wonder how I would have described my first step—and each one of those first steps....

The space between us felt so empty, yet also filled with possibilities, dreams, hopes, needs. Surrounding me, I sensed silent cheering and anticipation. My eyes were fixed on the open hands. I longed to reach them— only a few steps were needed.

I had enjoyed the embrace of those arms and hands; I'd been comforted by them; protected by them. Now, they were just out of my reach—but not too far; they were longer than mine—long enough to reach me. The silent cheering grew louder. The hands moved only slightly closer, but the rest was up to me. I had never moved in this way. I guess I was practicing for a new future—a different future. No more sitting on the sidelines and observing the world around me. They knew it was my time, and somehow, I knew it too. My rapid breaths supported my wildly pounding heart, even through my outstretched fingers. I needed help, yet somehow, I also knew that God had already equipped me to do this.

At first, I felt the void between us and thought I was far from Him. When I looked around, I realized I had been hearing His voice, sensing His direction, learning much from Him, experiencing His help and intervention—I just wasn't feeling His touch. Then I saw Him—delighting in me and drawing me to something new. I could also see that He was waiting for me at that new place, to embrace me, but I also knew that if I fell along the way, He was only HIS arm's length away to catch me.

Being a warrior for Jesus could be a completely new experience, or it could just include new experiences. Regardless, He cheers us on from our very first step through our very last. And He doesn't miss a single step.

As I am reading through the Bible in a year, the one theme I keep hearing over and over (and know, personally, to be true) is this: *Whatever you face in life, the very best thing you can do is to allow it to draw your heart to God.*

Unless my soul finds rest and peace in intimacy with Jesus in every different season, I will look for it in other activities and purposes that can never adequately fill the space—and I will remain restless. You and I can recognize the empty space and let it motivate us to take a step toward Him.

There have been many times in my life when I would have despaired if I hadn't had hope.

In some seasons, my circumstances felt discouraging to the point of despair, but then someone came along to help me carry my burdens or give me a glimpse of a better future. Sometimes God restored hope through the comfort of a pet or a garden full of flowers or a sunny day. But by far, my biggest source of hope has been this: "I would have despaired unless I had believed that I would see the goodness of the Lord in the land of the living." (Psalm 27.13) Take a step toward Him for hope.

EMBRACE THE SEASONS

I was sitting at a park asking God to speak to me. I noticed the tree in front of me and that the buds on it were just starting to appear. God's voice spoke to my heart:

There are seasons in your life that cause your leaves to drop and your branches to appear barren. Although life continues to respond with liveliness around you, there's been a space surrounding your soul that feels cold and dormant. That space surrounding your soul is accomplishing a purpose. It is able to kill off deadly spiritual diseases and parasites—currently unrecognizable organisms that, if left unattended, could wreak havoc.

But it is just a season. As the purpose is accomplished, that space surrounding your soul becomes warmed and more connected to the liveliness of your environmental surroundings. New life begins to evidence itself in your outlook and actions, much like the buds on this tree. There is hope and purpose in every season. Soon the season you're in now will gradually reveal brilliance in color, peaceful warmth and exciting activity. There will be a surge of growth and life that will seem uncontrollable. But don't discount or neglect the place where you are in this current season as you anticipate what's ahead. What is being accomplished in you at this very moment is invaluable and monumental. Treasure it from My hand.

Describe the season you're currently in. Is it cold and dormant? Are you experiencing a surge of growth? As you ask God about your current season, what do you sense Him speaking to your heart about the season you're in?

WHATEVER YOU FACE IN LIFE, THE VERY BEST THING YOU CAN DO IS TO ALLOW IT TO DRAW YOUR HEART TO GOD.

7

WATCH ME

"'I have given you an example to follow. Do as
I have done to you.'" –John 13.15, NLT

When Jesus said "'Follow me, and I will make you fishers of men'" (Matthew 4.19, ESV), I believe He was saying:

Come with Me, undistracted, and watch what I'm doing. Experience My love for you as I experience love from My Father. Watch and imitate all that I do as I practice Truth with a heart of compassion. I'll teach you all that I know about how to experience God's love and how to allow it to overflow back to God and into the lives of other people. When you do this, you will reach people with God's love. Stay close to Me so you can see all that I'm doing. Ask questions about what I'm doing so that you understand how to apply it to yourself and the situations I will lead you through. Start practicing these things while you're with Me. Then I'm going to have you go and do the same things—going out into the world and teaching others all that I've taught you.

He calls us to be followers (disciples), and He sends us to be messengers (apostles). He trains us as disciples to be apostles. But don't ever stop being a disciple.

THE GREATEST COMMANDMENTS

When we watch Jesus' interactions as we read through the four Gospels, we can see that He demonstrated what He taught—the two greatest commandments: Jesus chose to love God first, and He chose to love others after that. A warrior woman keeps those two things in the forefront of her mind. They shape her choices as she walks through every day. But she's only able to do this by having God's immense love for her inscribed in her heart. "We love because he first loved us." (1 John 4.19)

TEARS OF A TENDER HEART

It's a trait of Jesus and a trait of a beautiful warrior woman to have a tender heart that embraces the tears of others and is willing to offer tears to others. Your willingness to let someone experience their pain, allowing them to cry, is a tender gift. It is also a tender gift to cry in the presence of someone else.

My parents first took me to church when I was five years old. I remember having such a tender heart in my youth that being in the church service often brought me to tears. I remember feeling shame because of my tears—I thought I was odd. I didn't see others brought to tears. I still struggle with feeling shame when I'm brought to tears in a public setting, and even in small, more private settings. One thing I am learning about tears is that they're not just for me. My tears and your tears can be a tender gift to others around us. While they may make us feel vulnerable and weak, they can also empower us to help others feel not-so-alone. There are even times when our tears can give emotion that others have a need to experience or release for themselves.

I love that Jesus welcomed tears. He had been invited to dinner in the home of a Pharisee. While having dinner with this Pharisee, there was a woman who washed His feet with her tears (Luke 7.38), and He honored her because of it. He didn't feel uncomfortable by it, and He didn't do anything to stop her tears. He described it as a beautiful display of love. It's important to note that He didn't focus on the one with tears as much as He focused on the one without tears, suggesting that he should learn from her.

Jesus wept with others—He wept with Mary after Lazarus died. (John 11.33-36) His disciples saw Him grieving because of the pain in His heart. (Mark 14.33-34)

The apostle Paul also offered the gift of tears: "For I wrote you out of great distress and anguish of heart and with many tears, not to grieve you but to let you know the depth of my love for you." (2 Corinthians 2.4)

Charles Dickens wrote:

"Heaven knows we need never be ashamed of our tears, for they are rain upon the blinding dust of earth, overlying our hard hearts. I was better after I had cried, than before—more sorry, more aware of my own ingratitude, more gentle." (Dickens, *Great Expectations*)

In your example for others, let your tears comfort others, empower others, offer freedom for others, display your love for God and reveal tender love toward others.

As you consider the examples I've mentioned in this chapter, how do you feel about expressing this kind of tearful emotion in the presence of others? Spend some time journaling about the impact this might have on your heart as well as the hearts of others.

8

IN THE GAME

"The LORD is my shepherd, I lack nothing. ²He makes me lie down in green pastures, he leads me beside quiet waters, ³he refreshes my soul. He guides me along the right paths for his name's sake." –Psalm 23.1-3

"*L*ord, tell me what to do! Show me what You want me to do.*"*

When we're in challenging circumstances, we often want God to just tell us what to do. Sometimes God speaks very clearly. Other times, not so much. When it seems God is quiet and not directing us, we may feel frustrated, abandoned, hurt, angry, weak or hopeless. Our pleas may sound spiritual, yet if we don't get immediate answers, we may feel a sense of panic or frustration welling up in us. I'm beginning to recognize that in those times, I'm not pursuing God for Himself, nor is it my plan to be available for however He wants to use me in His plan. I'm, instead, seeking God for the purpose of having some semblance of control. It feels like things are out of control if I don't see my next move.

The questions start coming:

    o   *"What if God leaves me on the sidelines and doesn't put me in the game?"*

    o   *"What if I don't have purpose?"*

    o   *"What if I don't recognize my purpose?"*

As a kid, I played softball. I wasn't very good, but I loved to play. I loved batting the most, although I wasn't a very productive batter. When I was put in the game, I was put in right field because that's where the least action was. Most of the time, though, I was on the bench. To me, the bench was a place of shame—a place for those who played poorly.

The lie I internalized as truth was that sitting on the bench and not being actively in the game meant that I wasn't good enough—that my contribution would be more harmful than good. Waiting on God tends to feel the same way.

When I'm in a season where there's a pause in my ministry life, I get anxious. I want God to show me what He wants me to do. I want to be useful to Him. I want to be recognized as a valuable player. But I strongly sense that God wants me to know that there's purpose in the pause. And that if He has me sitting on the bench, it's not because I'm a poor player or inadequate. God makes us wait for His purpose. He loves to take the weak and show His great strength. He loves to take the small and conquer the giants. He loves to take the uneducated and pour His brilliance through them to confound the intelligent who don't acknowledge Him.

Had God been my softball coach, I imagine myself first on the field, probably at first base. With God as my coach, I would have been equipped with His power to play the game brilliantly as I constantly trusted Him for His power—completely aware that the excellent skill was not coming from my own ability, but His.

As I wait on the bench today, I'm hearing Him.

A QUIET HEART

One thing I'm hearing is:

Don't try to figure out My plan. Just listen and trust that I have a game plan in place. I'll let you know when it's your turn to join in. If you're paying attention and listening, you'll hear My voice when I call you into the game to fill the role and position I have for you.

Sometimes God is quiet. I wonder if He's quiet with direction sometimes because it's not so much that He wants the right action, but that He wants the right heart in my actions. I can tell my kids to unload the dishwasher and they may do it cheerfully or not-so-cheerfully. But when my kids know that it delights me when they unload the dishwasher without my direction, I know they've connected with my heart. That's when, by their attitude and their actions, they show that they know me and know what pleases me. They are doing it out of love for me.

It's the same with God. When we come back to a place of peaceful rest and worship, we're able to connect with His heart. From there, we move forward with a heart to love Him, experience His love for us and love others in the actions we choose.

CHOOSING TO GET IN THE GAME

It became abundantly clear that God wanted Moses to get in the game, but he wasn't all in. He came up with reasons that he couldn't do what God was leading him to do.

Beth Moore said, "Don't look for a leader. You are the leader. People are looking to you. Be deliberate. Make sure they see Jesus. We're not here all that long and then there's BLISS. Forever bliss. Till then, we're over our heads. But we can dang-well decide what kind of over-our-heads we're gonna be." (Moore, "Over Our Heads")

When God wants you to get in the game, GO! And be all in. He will provide anything you lack.

Have you had times when you've been on the bench in life, waiting? In what areas of your life are you waiting now?

What are you believing during the waiting?

What is one thing you can think of that you could do just to delight God?

How do you feel about being called into the game?

9

JUST SHOW UP

(DO I HAVE WHAT IT TAKES?)

> "'And who knows but that you have come to
> your royal position for such a time as this?'"
> –Esther 4.14

We all have days where something good happens and we feel a party going on inside of us. And we all have days where it's hard to just get out of bed in the morning—or afternoon. On those days, it's not the voices of people celebrating that we hear. Instead, it's the sound of a mob in our head closing in to attack. Each of us has unique circumstances impacting those voices, but the negative voices have a similar theme.

Lauren Daigle's song, "You Say", sums it up well. It begins:

*I keep fighting voices in my mind that say
I'm not enough.*

*Every single lie that tells me I will never
measure up.*

*Am I more than just the sum of every high
and every low?*

Remind me once again just who I am because I need to know.

Do you ever feel like it's a futile pursuit to escape those negative voices and live in freedom? When we confidently know who we are in Christ, we know that we are safe and secure in God's sovereignty. From that place of safety, we are free to live out our calling. We are free to live out who He created us to be.

There was a time when God told a man to speak to a powerful leader to set a nation free. That man responded with reasons why he couldn't do it. So God chose to use the voice of someone else. God told that same man to throw down his herder's staff in front of that powerful leader. He did, and that piece of wood turned into a snake. God told him to pick up the snake by the tail. When he did, it turned back into his staff.

Another time, Jesus told a lame man to get up and walk. He did. And yet another time, Jesus told someone to come to Him walking on the water, and when he had his focus on Jesus, he did. He walked on the water.

One time, a lowly, timid man from the weakest clan of Israel was called by God to be a military leader of 300 men and fight an oppressive army of 135,000. God called him "a mighty warrior" *before* he fought. Then God brought victory for the *mighty warrior*, defeating the oppressive army.

WE ARE FREE TO LIVE OUT OUR CALLING. WE ARE FREE TO LIVE OUT WHO HE CREATED US TO BE.

What do all these situations have in common? They were all ordinary people who showed up. When they showed up, God used them to do the impossible. God could use them not because of what *they* could do, but only when they allowed God to do the impossible through them.

On those days when I hear the mob closing in to attack my mind—the voices that say I'm not enough, I'll never measure up, life is just pointless—I look for God's reminders that He does the impossible. God does amazing things when I just show up.

There was another man who said to Jesus, "'I do believe; help me overcome my unbelief!'" (Mark 9.24) It is intriguing and amazing that Jesus can help us with our unbelief. Jesus helps me with my unbelief even when I don't believe that He can help me believe that I'm enough. Jesus helps me with my unbelief when I continue to question whether I measure up or that my life has meaning. Jesus increases my faith when I choose to let Him and ask Him to. No one else can do that. Jesus will increase our faith and intersect our lives in such a way that we will be able to experience life in a whole new way. We will then be able to fulfill our calling and know that we are enough.

We talked about Queen Esther earlier. Some might say she was a victim of circumstances. Her family had been uprooted and exiled from Jerusalem to Babylon. While she was a young girl, both of her parents died. After their death, she lived under the care of her cousin, Mordecai. When she was still a young woman, the king of Babylon banished his wife from the kingdom, became very angry, and imposed an irrevocable law throughout the empire that every man should be the ruler of his home and demand respect and obedience from his wife.

Afterward, the king decided he wanted a harem filled with the young, beautiful women from the land. He would choose a wife from them—whoever was the most favorable to him. Esther was one of those young women who was chosen for the harem.

Esther was not given a choice in her life circumstances. She did, however, have a choice in how she would respond. Esther found favor with this controlling king, and he chose her for his wife. Esther honored God with this favor by appealing to the king on behalf of her oppressed people. The king was about to kill her entire people when she asked for his mercy.

Esther showed up to use whatever power, position and ability God had given her. God knew how He had equipped her and for what purpose He had equipped her—"for such a time as this."

In what ways has God uniquely equipped you?

Lauren Daigle says, for her, it's music on stage.

For me, it's writing.

Consider your circumstances and where God might want to use you and equip you right now. Do you have opportunity to share in small groups? Do you have opportunity to teach? Has God given you the ability to sing, write, paint, do landscaping, hospitality, draw, sculpt, play an instrument, serve, cook, decorate, woodwork, research, give financially, open your home for others, run errands, defend the weak, reach out to someone, ...

What is it for you? Where does God have you right now to make a difference?

Just show up. God will use you to do the impossible. God will use you not because of what you can do, but because you have allowed Him to do the impossible through you.

OBSTACLES

"'In this world you will have trouble. But take heart!
I have overcome the world.'"
–John 16.33

The tension was high. The pressure intense. The bell rang and the gates opened. Several horses burst onto the track. It was 1973, and the stands were packed with over 134,000 spectators. Sham and Secretariat were rivaling for the Kentucky Derby win. But when the other horses took off, Sham hit his head on the starting gate and ripped out two teeth. He ran his race, though. Sham overcame obstacles and ran so impressively that he broke the Derby record by a fraction of a second. He did have another obstacle—Secretariat. Sham didn't receive the fanfare for his extraordinary accomplishment because Secretariat broke the same Derby record in the same race by a fraction of a second more than Sham did.

One of my longings in life, and maybe one of your longings too, is to run my race well. So often, though, I come across obstacles that seem to stand in the way of my winning. As a competitive swimmer for many years, my biggest competitor was myself. My biggest obstacle was overcoming my own weaknesses. It really didn't come down to who was swimming in the lane next to me and how well they were doing. It was about overcoming things that held me back previously.

I missed a couple practices before a big swim meet. I had the flu. I lost about five pounds in two days, and I had become weak and dehydrated. Then we had the swim meet. I was determined to go and to do my best with no idea if I would even have the strength to finish. I swam my event. I did the best I could. When I finished my race, I looked up at my time, and I realized I had accomplished my best time ever in that event. I don't know what place I came in. That's not what it was about. I just wanted to run (or swim) my race well, and I did. That's what mattered. That was my victory.

As you look at your life, what obstacles are you facing? What is trying to hold you back? Once you recognize those things, then identify how you can overcome those obstacles so you can run your race impressively, becoming better than you were before.

A MIRROR

My husband and I had been playing a board game. When we first started playing it, I enjoyed the friendly competition. But then my attitude started turning sour. Part of the game allowed for an opponent to steal or invade space. I found that as long as I was able to run my own race without obstacles, I was okay, but my attitude began to turn ugly whenever obstacles (stealing or space invasion) prevented me from running my race as I desired.

After several experiences of my souring attitude, I thought it might be good for me to take a game break and examine my attitude. Maybe my response to the game was a mirror helping me see more clearly my response to similar circumstances in life.

I identified an underlying subtle demand for life to work as I wanted. John 16.33 says, "'In this world you will have trouble. But take heart! I have overcome the world.'" I wasn't living like I believe that. I want to live in a way that reflects my understanding that there WILL be obstacles. I also want to live in a way that reflects a belief that God will overcome obstacles and provide victory in unexpected ways, trusting that He has overcome the world.

On a scale of 1 to 10, indicate to what extent you believe the words of John 16.33 in the paragraph above.

Will you ask God to increase your faith in this area?

Take some time to journal about what you think it means where Jesus says, "I have overcome the world."

What impact does that have on your life?

HOPE FROM SUFFERING

One beautiful way we can give others hope in the midst of their obstacles is by our approach to suffering. Charles Dickens wrote:

"Suffering has been stronger than all other teaching…. I have been bent and broken, but – I hope – into a better shape." (Dickens: *Great Expectations*)

Take a moment right now to share with God what you see as your obstacles. Then ask Him to help you trust Him with the obstacles and suffering you face. Ask Him to overcome them and provide victory, possibly in unexpected ways.

Sit with women who sit at the feet of Jesus. The conversations are different. You walk away feeling inspired not inferior because those are the women who know this Christian walk is a race, but not a competition.

11

WE ARE DUSTY

"'Take my yoke upon you and learn from me,
for I am gentle and humble in heart,
and you will find rest for your souls.'"
–Matthew 11.29

Dave Barnes has a song called, "Carry Me Through". Part of it says, "Oh, Lord, be gentle 'cause I'm just a man. Please don't crush me with Your heavenly hand."

We are fragile. We are made from dust into clay pots that can be easily broken. I was given a new coffee mug. I put some hot water in it to make myself some tea. A few minutes later, I noticed water seeping through a tiny crack, creating a puddle of water beneath the mug. It's fragile and easily breakable.

We, too, are easily breakable. Before I was born, my mom experienced intense pain. Several different times over the course of a few weeks, believing she was in labor, she went to the hospital. She was sent home from the Emergency Room several times because she wasn't actually in labor. The medical staff didn't realize her appendix was about to burst, which felt to her like labor pains. It wasn't until immediately after I was born that they recognized the appendicitis. It was a miracle that her appendix hadn't burst and taken both of our lives. The fact that we are made of dust and filled with breath from God, and that we can maintain life for 80 years or so, is truly a miraculous thing.

That song, "Carry Me Through", is a good reminder that my life is just a vapor that is completely dependent on God's care: His breath in me, His maintenance of my body temperature, His provision of what my body needs to heal itself, His rhythm that keeps my heart beating in the right time, and other intricacies that I'm either only vaguely familiar with or not even cognizant of at all. Without this kind of care from Him, I'd be immediately crushed and returned to dust.

As a warrior, I recognize that I am dependent on God for life when I run into each battle. I also need to stay aligned with Him in the way I battle in the midst of all of God's creation. They are dusty too.

REFLECT GENTLENESS

God builds us up to be effective warriors. He understands that we are just clay pots made of dust. He binds up the brokenhearted, and He shapes us with love, tenderness, joy and peace. He builds us with faithfulness, patience, goodness, kindness, self-control—qualities that are never selfishly focused and never irritable. Without these virtuous qualities, we would only hear noise. God's default is always gentleness.

In 1 Corinthians 4.21, Paul says to a repeatedly rebellious and sinful church, "Shall I come to you with a rod of discipline, or shall I come in love and with a gentle spirit?" Paul's default was gentleness, but there were occasions for calculated discipline with love, taking into consideration who the recipient was, the condition of their heart and how they might learn and grow.

God's default is to use His power and authority for healing. We often see people in this world using power and authority in destructive ways, trying to get ahead or make life work the way they want. Sometimes even to get others to do what's right. Although His rule is gentleness, God uses carefully calculated exceptions to determine when He needs to burn off impurity. It's after He's given many warnings and opportunities for repentance.

There have been times when I've been approached with harshness in my brokenness. It caused me to want to run away, even though my desire was to want to be drawn toward change.

Where have you had those experiences where you needed to change but harshness pushed you further away?

HOW TO APPROACH DUST

Imagine two heaps of dust battling each other. That's what it is to fight flesh with flesh or attempt to shut others down. That's what happened with the first brothers in the Bible. Cain was angry because of jealousy toward Abel. Cain responded with harshness, murdering his brother. Jesus said when you are angry with your brother, it's likened to murder. The enemy's tactic is to get us to fight each other. He tries to set us against each other. When we recognize that we are in this together as heaps of dust that could easily sweep each other away, we'll be better able to bind up the brokenhearted. We'll be more equipped to lovingly challenge, encourage, strengthen and sharpen one another. We'll be better able to get behind one another and support each other, lifting each other up. As we grow in discerning needs and understanding how to approach one another in our battles, our hearts will be developed for more effective battle.

A warrior's default is to wield her sword with skillful gentleness. Sounds like an oxymoron, doesn't it? But isn't that how God typically works? He says when we are weak, then we are strong. When we yoke ourselves to Christ, we find freedom. When we delight in God, He fulfills our desires. The last will be first, and the least is the greatest.

There's a beautiful scene in the movie, *Redeeming Love*, based on the book by Francine Rivers, written as an adaptation of the Bible's book of Hosea. In the movie, it's the 1800s, and Angel has married Michael in an attempt to flee her life of prostitution. But when she realizes she doesn't know how to live a normal life, she quietly leaves their home. Without him knowing, she sets out to walk the twenty miles back into the town of her familiar lifestyle. A mile down the dirt road, Michael approaches on horseback. She sees him and turns to him to sharply remark that she doesn't want to be married to him. He silently gets off his horse, hands her water and a coat and then tells her she'll need these for the journey. He gently offers her a choice: to walk 19 miles to a life that will destroy her or turn around and walk one mile to her home, where she will be cherished by her husband who loves her. He quietly turns around, gets on his horse and rides home. Hours later and worn out from walking, she stumbles in the door of their small house and sits down in a chair, seemingly defeated and ashamed. He silently walks toward her with a basin and water. He kneels down, carefully removes her shoes from her blistered feet and gently washes her feet.

Love is always invitational. Love redeems.

How has God approached and redeemed you in His gentleness to develop you into a better warrior?

WHAT A WARRIOR DOES

12

PICK UP YOUR SHIELD

"take up the shield of faith."
–Ephesians 6.16

A warrior woman has amazing pieces of armor. There's one that is certainly a defensive piece, yet it is very much an offensive piece as well—the shield. Ephesians 6.16 alludes to the defensive aspect of it: "take up the shield of faith, with which you can extinguish all the flaming arrows of the evil one." Our faith or trust in God, believing what He says, will protect us from the lies, deceit, confusion and traps of the enemy.

But that's not all the shield does. 1 Timothy 6.12 (NASB) says to "Fight the good fight of faith." This verse guides us in where to direct our battle. A major part of our battle is to establish our faith in such a way that when the enemy attacks, we are already prepared with a strong shield of faith. Offensively developing our faith is the good fight that will ensure that we are prepared when our faith is most needed. That shield will provide us with protection of peace and joy over turmoil and fear. Our shield of faith will provide us with the ability to love instead of our natural tendency to seek revenge or be cold toward someone in a conflict situation. It will give us the ability to practice patience, kindness and goodness when we might otherwise be tempted to be frustrated, self-righteous and self-centered. It will help us to be faithful when we're tired. It helps us to be gentle when it would be easier to react without much thought. It gives us self-control when we would rather demand fairness, or when our flesh is hungering for what it feels is lacking.

I know many of you reading this have experienced various degrees of childhood pain or trauma. Maybe one of your parents wasn't emotionally available. Maybe one of them caused physical harm to you. It can be devastating to a child when a parent doesn't fulfill his or her role as God intended. That child carries that pain into adulthood. Was that one of your parents? Did you feel scared, unsafe emotionally, unprotected, uncared for? Were you left with an emotional void? Maybe you didn't have anyone to help you through what you were feeling—the fear, the confusion, the loneliness, the uncertainty. Maybe it led to beliefs that you've carried through your whole life:

- o   *I'm not safe.*
- o   *I'm not cared for.*
- o   *I'm not emotionally protected.*

What's the truth?

I wonder how you would respond if God spoke this to you:

> *When your dad pushed you aside, I caught you. I broke your fall so you wouldn't be hurt. When you went and hid behind the door, listening to his angry outbursts from a distance, I sat with you. When you watched your mom take those drugs and then drink the alcohol and pass out on the couch, I'm the one that let a friend*

know—I'm the one that had her come to care for you. When you needed a safe place to run to, I'm the one that prompted that unexpected caring person to provide a place of respite for you. I provided the animals you loved so that you wouldn't be alone, so that you would have a source of physical AND emotional comfort to get through those difficult years.

But know this—your parents weren't the enemy. Your parents didn't make you feel alone or unprotected, unsafe or uncared for. They felt all those same things, and you saw how they responded to their own painful feelings. Your enemy (and their enemy) is the one who convinced each of you of the lies that perpetuated pain for each of you. Satan convinced all of you and used you against each other. He set you up to make you enemies, when, in fact, he is the source of your pain—your true enemy.

Your battle is not against flesh and blood.

1 Timothy 1.19 in the Message translation says:

"All those prayers are coming together now so you will do this well, fearless in your struggle, keeping a firm grip on your faith and on yourself. After all, this is a fight we're in."

Are you keeping a firm grip on your faith? What does that look like for you?

The Bible says to be on the alert because Satan roams around like a roaring lion looking for someone to devour. Sometimes we are weak, fearful or struggling with something. He is drawn to it and sends a whole pride of lions to try to finish us off. Be aware of Satan's schemes. Hold onto your faith in God. Hold onto the joy that is a result of your faith. We don't have to let Satan steal our joy or our faith because our God is stronger and has already promised us victory.

How do we pick up our shield and grow our faith?

I think of the man who said to Jesus, "'I do believe; help me overcome my unbelief.'" (Mark 9.24) God loves those prayers and is ready to increase our faith when we come to Him that way. Prayer—just having conversations with God—builds our relationship with Him and our faith.

What is an area of your life where you believe but also have some unbelief? Will you tell God about it and ask Him to increase your faith? It will be a shield for you.

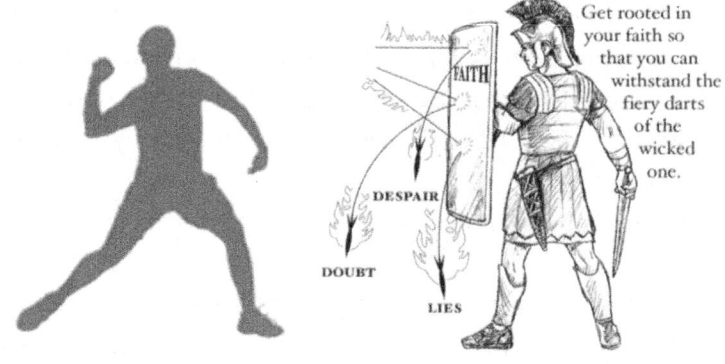

Get rooted in your faith so that you can withstand the fiery darts of the wicked one.

FAITH

DESPAIR

DOUBT

LIES

A MAJOR PART OF OUR BATTLE IS TO ESTABLISH OUR FAITH IN SUCH A WAY THAT WHEN THE ENEMY ATTACKS, WE ARE ALREADY PREPARED WITH A STRONG SHIELD.

13

LAUGH

> "'... the joy of the Lord is your strength.'"
> –Nehemiah 8.10b

My daughter and I were at home, each working late into the night. We took a break and began looking through some old journals that I kept where I had written down funny stories and cute things that each of my kids did or said. We laughed and laughed, and then we were energized from the laughter. It was just a break we took, but with the energy it gave us, we felt like we could stay up all night.

The next day, we slept in. Once we got our day started, I pulled out a few more stories. Again, our laughter filled the house to the point where my husband came out to see what was so entertaining.

As we read the stories that reflected God's faithfulness, goodness and presence in our family, it brought us delight. And that in turn gave us energy and strength.

The Bible tells us that the joy of the Lord is our strength. But is it really? We can see that it's true when it's easy to laugh in our circumstances, but what about in trials?

Oftentimes, I look for strength to get through my trials, but any strength I find feels so fleeting. I actually have a choice about what I stand under in trying times. I can choose to stand under my trial, or I can choose to stand under the joy of the Lord.

What do you stand under in trying times?

Nehemiah 8.10 says, "The joy of the Lord is your strength." Are you standing under the joy of the Lord to get your strength? Or are you trying to beg for or muster up strength as you stand under a trial, with the burden of that challenging situation weighing you down?

If I'm honest, I spend a lot of time standing under the trial. I'll focus on the trial, obsess about the trial, strategize and even pray about my trial, trying to get strength to endure my trial. And the more I focus on it, the more lost I feel.

At times I wonder, if the joy of the Lord is truly my strength, then why is my focus on that trial?

One of my life verses has repeatedly rescued me:

"Don't worry about anything; instead, pray about everything. Tell God what you need, and thank him for all he has done. Then you will experience God's peace...." (Philippians 4.6-7a, NLT)

Why not pray about the trial and tell God what I need? Why not ask others to pray about it, and then focus on what God has done in the past? Remember His faithfulness and goodness in the past. Remember all the fruit of the spirit that naturally flows from Him: love, joy, peace, patience, kindness, goodness, faithfulness, gentleness and self-control.

GRACE

When I looked up the word "grace" at dictionary.com, one definition said, "The influence or spirit of God operating in humans to regenerate or strengthen them."

Another website says:

> The Greek word *charis* is used 122 times in the New Testament when it is translated "grace". This word can also be translated "thanks", such as in 2 Corinthians 9:15, "Thanks be to God for His indescribable gift!" God's goodness is so closely tied up with joy that thanksgiving is wrapped around it from beginning to the end. A close word to *charis* is *chara* which means joy. Whenever anyone treats us with favor, we are filled with joy and naturally respond with thanksgiving. (Foundations)

Grace will naturally result in joy. In other words, joy reflects our experience of grace. When we focus on God's favor, His grace toward us, the natural result will be joy. We'll soon be praising Him and sensing His joy welling up in us to the point that we can't contain it. That joy will bring strength. When we then look over at the trial, we can face whatever is needed. Then we can turn back and keep our eyes on God's faithfulness and goodness in all that He's done.

When we experience God's peace and joy, it will overflow to others.

[10]Nehemiah said, "Go and enjoy choice food and sweet drinks, and send some to those who have nothing prepared. This day is holy to our Lord. Do not grieve, for the joy of the Lord is your strength."

[11]The Levites calmed all the people, saying, "Be still, for this is a holy day. Do not grieve."

[12]Then all the people went away to eat and drink, to send portions of food and to celebrate with great joy, because they now understood the words that had been made known to them. (Nehemiah 8.10-12)

Take time today to journal and remember all God has done. And laugh—our hearts need it.

A CHEERFUL HEART IS
GOOD MEDICINE.
-PROVERBS 17.22

14

DON'T LAUGH

(SARAH)

"'Why did Sarah laugh...?'"
–Genesis 18.13

There is a time to laugh and a time to refrain from laughter. Abraham's wife, Sarah, laughed, but it wasn't a good choice. Genesis 18.10-15 describes her dilemma.

Then one of them said, "I will surely return to you about this time next year, and Sarah your wife will have a son."

Now Sarah was listening at the entrance to the tent, which was behind him. ¹¹Abraham and Sarah were already very old, and Sarah was past the age of childbearing. ¹²So Sarah laughed to herself as she thought, "After I am worn out and my lord is old, will I now have this pleasure?"

¹³Then the Lord said to Abraham, "Why did Sarah laugh and say, 'Will I really have a child, now that I am old?' ¹⁴Is anything too hard for the Lord? I will return to

you at the appointed time next year, and Sarah will have a son."

¹⁵Sarah was afraid, so she lied and said, "I did not laugh."

But he said, "Yes, you did laugh."

Being a warrior woman requires that we believe what God says and trust His timing. He will always speak truth to us. Sarah laughed at the news that she would have a baby, but she also knew that she and her husband were both old and worn out. I notice, as I read their story, that the "man" knew her thoughts as if she had said it out loud (verse 12). I find it interesting that Abraham also laughed at the news in the previous chapter. I don't know what the difference was between Abraham's and Sarah's laughter, but I wonder if his laughter was a response of, *Wow! I know you really could do this if you wanted, but it seems more practical for Ishmael to be the offspring that would make me the father of many nations.*

I wonder if Sarah's laughter was a reaction of, *Ha! He is really mistaken on this one. Doesn't he (He) realize that is impossible? Or possibly, Doesn't he (He) realize the timing's bad?* Sarah's laughter seemed to communicate disbelief in what God intended to do. God is the One who accomplishes things that are unlikely, so it makes sense for Him to choose to do the impossible (rather than the possible) through us. The Bible is full of examples of God accomplishing the impossible through people:

➢ Jesus being born of a virgin (Luke 1)
➢ Daniel being thrown in a den of hungry lions and not being touched by them. (Daniel 6)

- Shadrach, Meshach and Abednego surviving being thrown in a blazing furnace and not even smelling like smoke. (Daniel 3)
- A small boy killing a champion warrior giant with a small stone in a slingshot. (1 Samuel 17)
- Gideon defeating an army of 135,000 with his own army of 300. (Judges 8)
- Jesus raising Lazarus from the dead. (John 11)
- King Jehoshaphat's army being victorious against three other more powerful armies just by standing still. (2 Chronicles 20)
- Peter walking on water (Matthew 14)

We hear these stories, but when it comes to our own lives, we often look at our circumstances and determine that it's impossible for us, and we stop there. We respond like Sarah, concluding that it's ridiculous to think I can have a baby at my age. Or it's crazy to continue to stay in this marriage that would be impossible to endure. It's preposterous to imagine forgiving that person whose sin toward me was devastating. Maybe I believe that one thing I'm addicted to will always control me and I'll never be able to change. Maybe I've always struggled with identity issues and have never been comfortable with my gender so I know I will always be this way.

Don't be surprised when God calls you to do the impossible. Don't be surprised when He calls you to get out of the boat and walk on the water. God is not suggesting that you have the power to do it; He's suggesting that He can do it through you. He's the One who will bring the results.

Sarah's story doesn't end with her unbelief.

Now the Lord was gracious to Sarah as he had said, and the Lord did for Sarah what he had promised. [2]Sarah became pregnant and bore a son to Abraham in his old age, at the very time God had promised him. [3]Abraham gave the name Isaac to the son Sarah bore him. [4]When his son Isaac was eight days old, Abraham circumcised him, as God commanded him. [5]Abraham was a hundred years old when his son Isaac was born to him.

[6]Sarah said, "God has brought me laughter, and everyone who hears about this will laugh with me." (Genesis 21.1-6)

Sarah's cynical laughter of disbelief turned to laughter of joy that she would then share beautifully with others. Just like Sarah, there's hope for us too when we've been unbelieving. We can choose now to believe, and He will faithfully pour out His grace... and joy.

Is there something in your life right now that is hard to believe God would do for you? Take some time to journal about it.

HE'S THE ONE WHO WILL BRING
THE RESULTS.

15

PICK UP YOUR SWORD
(IDENTIFYING THE BATTLE)

"the sword of the Spirit, which is the word of God."
–Ephesians 6.17

After listening to a teaching, I thought how good the sermon was—the pastor used illustrations to help us apply the Word of God to our lives. Scripture was prevalent throughout his teaching, and I walked away thinking how good that was for my spirit to hear, and I went on with my day. But then I stopped. I sensed conviction in my spirit.

God wasn't leading me to look at or inspect someone else's sword. He leads me to pick up my own sword. Just like young David couldn't defeat a Philistine giant with Saul's sword, neither can we defeat our opposition without knowing God's Word for ourselves and applying it to our lives as He guides us.

I am able to get God's Word into my mind by studying it for myself. I am able to get God's Word into my heart by meditating on it—consciously asking God how it applies to me and taking time to listen as He speaks in my spirit. God sometimes speaks in my thoughts or through my circumstances. He always reveals truth that aligns with what I read in His Word. He empowers me to use His Word in and through my life in this way.

A warrior woman has a tough responsibility as she picks up her sword and looks out on the world. She must carefully discern the battle—keenly aware that our battle is not against flesh and blood, but also aware that flesh and blood are impacted by the battle.

The Bible says the sword is the Word of God. How do we use the Word of God to battle?

KNOW YOUR MISSION

My cousin is a police officer. He has also had SWAT training. His SWAT team often enters dangerous situations to rescue someone. They arrive on the scene with weapons prepared. If they can accomplish the mission of rescuing the person in question with no confrontation with others or violence, that's what they do. They engage their weapons only when a situation requires it to successfully accomplish the mission.

In whatever situation I find myself, it's good to remember my mission and my goals. Some questions to ask when I step into what sometimes seems to be a battlefield:

+ What is my mission?
+ What is God calling me to do/accomplish right now?
+ How can I respond in a helpful, God-honoring way?
+ Is my criticism necessary, constructive and beneficial?

As we consider our mission, what then is the role of God's Word in that mission?

> ...the Holy Scriptures, which are able to make you wise for salvation through faith in Christ Jesus. All Scripture is God-breathed and is useful for teaching, rebuking, correcting and training in righteousness, so that the servant of God may be thoroughly equipped for every good work. (2 Timothy 3.15-17)

The sword of God's Word allows us to teach (instruct). It allows us to rebuke (address rebellion). It allows us to correct (guide in a different direction). And it allows us to train in righteousness (shape in holy living those who are willing, including ourselves), perfectly equipping us for every good work. I like the wording of The Message translation:

> "Every part of Scripture is God-breathed and useful one way or another—showing us truth, exposing our rebellion, correcting our mistakes, training us to live God's way. Through the Word we are put together and shaped up for the tasks God has for us." (2 Timothy 3.15-17, MSG)

In order to identify the battle and use our sword effectively, we need to be very familiar with our sword—study the Word, listen to wise teaching regarding the Word, and practice applying it to our own life. When we're familiar with it and have it stored in our heart, God will faithfully bring it to mind when we need it.

What truth is God showing you today?

Is His Word exposing any hint of rebellion in your heart right now?

Are you heading in a direction in some part of your life that is veering off God's path for you?

Are there any other ways that you can see God training or shaping you right now?

16

DROP YOUR SWORD

"For when I am weak, then I am strong."
—2 Corinthians 12.10

CRY AND BE STRONG

S ometimes it's good to cry. Sometimes we stay strong and in control of our emotions, when instead, we may really need to cry and release the emotion that has built up.

I arrived at my hotel room for a writing week where I intended to compile four years' worth of notes for this book. I took a moment and closed my eyes and listened. What surfaced was weariness and a need to just (as Twila Paris stated in a song many years ago) "drop my sword and cry for just awhile, 'cause deep inside this armor, the warrior is a child." I believe I do need to be strong. God often gave the command to be strong to those He was calling to leadership, to those who were fearful, and to His people in general.

➢ To Joshua: "'Be strong and courageous. Do not be afraid; do not be discouraged, for the Lord your God will be with you wherever you go.'" –Joshua 1.9

➢ To Israel through Moses: "'Be strong and courageous. Do not be afraid or terrified because of them, for the Lord your God goes with you; he will never leave you nor forsake you.'" –Deuteronomy 31.6

➢ King David to Solomon: "'Consider now, for the Lord has chosen you to build a house as the sanctuary. Be strong and do the work.'" –1 Chronicles 28.10

➢ To Asa, all Judah and Benjamin through Azariah: "'But as for you, be strong and do not give up, for your work will be rewarded.'" –2 Chronicles 15.7

➢ To the people of Judah through Hezekiah: "'Be strong and courageous. Do not be afraid or discouraged because of the king of Assyria and the vast army with him, for there is a greater power with us than with him. With him is only the arm of flesh, but with us is the Lord our God to help us and to fight our battles.' And the people gained confidence from what Hezekiah the king of Judah said." –2 Chronicles 32.7-8

➢ To the fearful through Isaiah: "'Be strong, do not fear; your God will come, he will come with vengeance; with divine retribution he will come to save you.'" –Isaiah 35.4

➢ To Daniel through an angel of the Lord (Gabriel): "'Do not be afraid, you who are highly esteemed,' he said. 'Peace! Be strong now; be strong.'" –Daniel 10.19

➢ To Zerubbabel, Joshua son of Jozadak and all the people of the land through Haggai: "'But now be strong, Zerubbabel,' declares the Lord. 'Be strong, Joshua son of Jozadak, the high priest. Be strong all you people of the land,' declares the Lord, 'and work. For I am with you,' declares the Lord Almighty. 'This is what I covenanted with you when you came out of Egypt. And my Spirit remains among you. Do not fear.'" –Haggai 2.4-5

When I'm told to be strong, my first instinct is to push down tender emotions and muster up every ounce of energy I can find. But the Bible presents a different image of strength.

Being strong requires being authentic. It requires revealing our fears and our tears and being authentically weak so that there's room for us to be filled with God's strength. "That is why, for Christ's sake, I delight in weaknesses, in insults, in hardships, in persecutions, in difficulties. For when I am weak, then I am strong." (2 Corinthians 12.10)

I love that I can drop my sword and rest while Jesus manages all the battles going on. Since it doesn't depend on me, but on Him, I can rest securely in His peace and care. And in the rest, He will renew my strength.

Where in your life right now do you feel weak? Imagine God infusing that area of your life with His strength. Describe what that looks like.

Where in your life right now do you sense emotion has built up and you just need to cry? Will you allow yourself time and space to cry? Release the tears and let God hold them for you.

"You have seen me tossing and turning through the night. You have collected all my tears and preserved them in your bottle! You have recorded every one in your book." (Psalm 56.8, TLB)

"I cling to you; your strong right hand holds me securely." (Psalm 63.8, NLT)

17

SLEEP

(AT THE RIGHT TIME)

"Jesus was sleeping at the back of the boat
with his head on a cushion."
–Mark 4.38, NLT

The disciples were in the boat with Jesus. There was chaos surrounding them—a storm was tossing the boat, the waves were high and dangerous, and the disciples thought they were going to die. What was Jesus doing? Sleeping.

Do you sometimes feel like you're in a boat that's filling with water and you're about to drown—and Jesus is sleeping?

Why in the world would Jesus be sleeping at such a crazy, chaotic time? I'm sure that's what the disciples were wondering too.

35As evening came, Jesus said to his disciples, "Let's cross to the other side of the lake." 36So they took Jesus in the boat and started out, leaving the crowds behind (although other boats followed). 37But soon a fierce storm came up. High waves were breaking into the boat, and it began to fill with water.

³⁸Jesus was sleeping at the back of the boat with his head on a cushion. The disciples woke him up, shouting, "Teacher, don't you care that we're going to drown?"

³⁹When Jesus woke up, he rebuked the wind and said to the waves, "Silence! Be still!" Suddenly the wind stopped, and there was a great calm. ⁴⁰Then he asked them, "Why are you afraid? Do you still have no faith?" (Mark 4.35-40, NLT)

Jesus was able to sleep because He was at peace. He knew that nothing would overtake His life apart from God's sovereign plan. Jesus knew He didn't have to fear the waves, because the waves had to listen to Him. He also understood that, in His human form, His body, like ours, required rest. Apparent chaos didn't prevent Jesus from sleeping at the right time.

Does chaos keep you from sleeping when you need rest? No matter how fierce the storms are in our lives, like Jesus, we can rest, confident that nothing can overtake our lives apart from His sovereign plan.

. . . .

"So the captain went down after him. 'How can you sleep at a time like this?' he shouted. 'Get up and pray to your god! Maybe he will pay attention to us and spare our lives.'" (Jonah 1.6, NLT)

Jonah wasn't sleeping at the right time. It sounds to me like his sleeping was an escape; maybe a form of denial—the same way he was trying to escape God's direction for him to go to Ninevah.

Is there something you want to escape? Do you pursue sleep to avoid it? Just like Jesus has power over external chaos, He also has power for your internal chaos.

. . . .

[36]Then Jesus went with his disciples to a place called Gethsemane, and he said to them, "Sit here while I go over there and pray." [37]He took Peter and the two sons of Zebedee along with him, and he began to be sorrowful and troubled. [38]Then he said to them, "My soul is overwhelmed with sorrow to the point of death. Stay here and keep watch with me."

[39]Going a little farther, he fell with his face to the ground and prayed, "My Father, if it is possible, may this cup be taken from me. Yet not as I will, but as you will."

[40]Then he returned to his disciples and found them sleeping. "Couldn't you men keep watch with me for one hour?" he asked Peter. [41]"Watch and pray so that you will not fall into temptation. The spirit is willing, but the flesh is weak."

[42]He went away a second time and prayed, "My Father, if it is not possible for this cup to be taken away unless I drink it, may your will be done."

[43]When he came back, he again found them sleeping, because their eyes were heavy. [44]So he left them and went away once more and prayed the third time, saying the same thing.

[45]Then he returned to the disciples and said to them, "Are you still sleeping and resting? Look, the

hour has come, and the Son of Man is delivered into the hands of sinners. ⁴⁶Rise! Let us go! Here comes my betrayer!" (Matthew 26.36-46)

There is a time to sleep and a time to stay awake. It may take discernment to know which is best. Jesus had given them direction to stay awake the first time. When they failed the first time, He explained why they should stay awake: so they wouldn't fall into temptation. And yet they still fell asleep again. Sometimes staying awake isn't just about not sleeping—it could also mean staying vigilant about the things that can tempt us.

When you sit down to have focused time with God, do you tend to try to find answers? Do you try to figure out what you should read or what God has for you to do next? Those are good questions, but do you know that sometimes it's okay to just rest with Him?

"'Come to me, all you who are weary and burdened, and I will give you rest.'" (Matthew 11.28)

I like the wording of the Amplified Bible, Classic Edition:

"'Come to Me, all you who labor and are heavy-laden and overburdened, and I will cause you to rest. [I will ease and relieve and refresh your souls.]'" (AMPC)

Can you sit back and rest your head right now? Take some deep breaths and share your heart with the Lord. Let Him "ease and relieve and refresh your soul". Give your chaos to Him, and rest peacefully as God leads.

18

THAW OUT

"'For the wedding of the Lamb has come, and his bride
has made herself ready.'"
–Revelation 19.7

ESCAPING FROZEN:
(MOTIVATION DURING A WORLD-WIDE CRISIS)

That morning, my heart and mind were flooded with social media comments. People were feeling "frozen", lacking motivation, feeling scared and depressed. They didn't feel like getting out of their pajamas, and they were glued to news channels. I certainly get that. For the first week of staying in during a world-wide quarantine, I felt many of those things. My attention was captivated by what was happening in our world. I was completely thrown out of my routine, and control of my own life was being overtaken daily. My normal activities of running errands and connecting with people at coffee shops were thwarted, and it left me feeling frozen and lacking motivation.

The second week was different. I may have needed the downtime of the first week to absorb the shock and grief throughout the world, but I knew I didn't want to stay in that frozen place. I made the choice to put my phone down and take time away from media. But I also knew that, even in a time of disruption, I still wanted my life to make a difference.

I was encouraged by those who found ways to use their gifts for others. Many musicians offered their gifts to others through Facebook watch parties. Some comedians did the same. One of my gifts is writing, but I found that when I felt frozen, I couldn't write. I needed to find a way to "thaw out."

What makes you feel frozen? How do you respond to those frozen feelings? I've found it helpful to take baby steps to embrace purpose and move beyond frozen feelings. Here are some things that help me to thaw when I feel frozen:

REMEMBERING I AM THE BRIDE OF CHRIST

My husband accepts me no matter how I look, but when I take time to look good (inside and out), it delights him. At our wedding, I didn't show up to meet my groom in my pajamas. I took time to look beautiful for him.

Jesus accepts me regardless of how I look, but I would really like to delight Him by caring for my outward appearance as well as my inner existence. My outward appearance is impacted by care for my inner existence. My inner existence is beautified as I spend time with Jesus and in His Word. I share my thoughts and feelings with Him and listen as He speaks to me through His Word. I prepare myself each day, both internally and externally, to present myself as the bride of Christ. Even if no one else sees me, I am prepared for Him. But I'm also prepared for this new era of video calls and video meetings—I just never know when I'll get one of those surprise calls these days.

GETTING THE ARMOR OUT OF THE CLOSET

God has clearly shown me that He's given me armor. But am I really wearing the armor that He's provided for me? Or is it just hanging in my closet? I ask myself some questions to help me determine whether or not I'm wearing my armor:

> ➤ Have I gotten lax in taking my thoughts captive?
> ➤ Am I trusting Him to give me peace in staying away from the areas where I should not go?
> ➤ Am I saturating my mind with truth from God's Word?
> ➤ Am I leaning on God throughout each day to save me from every area where I fall short?
> ➤ Am I recognizing that my enemy in each day is not flesh and blood?
> ➤ Am I trusting God's sovereignty, provision and power?

God has given me an amazing privilege by giving me armor, but His provision of armor requires that I actually put it on.

MAKING A 'TO DO' LIST

Having a lack of structure feeds the frozen feeling. I find that when I plan out my day with a To Do List, it gives me goals and structure. I try to keep as much normalcy in my days as I can, so when I get up (in the morning!), here are the first things I personally try to do regularly:

• Wake and check for any messages to add to my To Do List (that I wrote out the night before) for the day.
• Walk to the kitchen and heat up some filtered water.
• Add warm water to my glass water bottle, along with sea salt and a drop of lemon oil.

- Take my iodine supplement and probiotic with my warm water.
- A few times each week, walk on my treadmill while I listen to an inspirational teaching (or possibly walk later in the day).
- Shower and prepare myself physically to present myself as the bride of Christ—as I also spend time thinking, praying and listening with Jesus while I'm getting myself ready for the day. Some days I will also spend some time stretching (with or without weights) either before, in the middle of or after getting ready.
- Go back to the kitchen to eat something (e.g., some berries and some nuts OR I will make a smoothie in my blender using a banana, frozen berries, nuts, protein powder and several other things).
- Take my other vitamins (with more warm water).
- Sit down for a little while to connect with God—maybe reading, writing, singing, reflecting, listening, sharing (presenting requests, fears, joys, sadness, confusion, gratitude). Every encounter is different for time and content, but then I also communicate with Him constantly throughout the day as I go through the day.
- Oftentimes, that time connecting with Him provides the structure and content I need to shape the rest of my day. Then I begin to do other things on my To Do List.

Your day won't begin exactly like mine, and even my mornings aren't always in the same order, but consider what you can do to provide some normalcy and structure to your own day to help you to live out your role as the bride of Christ. As you do that, you'll begin to thaw out and escape frozen feelings.

19

IMPACT

(RUTH)

> "'Why have I found such favor in your eyes that you notice me—a foreigner?'" –Ruth 2.10

I never wanted to make waves or disrupt people's lives. But now I see the value in living in such a way that I do impact people's lives in ways that cause them to change for good. One small example is in cooking. I choose to eat healthy. I could keep my own food in my own little bubble and then make other food for my family or, with sensitivity to preferences, I can let my style of eating healthy overflow into the lives of those around me. They can choose if they want to eat it, but it will be accessible for positive impact in their lives.

I was reading in the book of Ruth. It's possible that Ruth never knew her father-in-law. He died before she married for the first time. Ruth did, however, know her mother-in-law, Naomi, for about ten years before Ruth's own husband died. At that point, Naomi decided to return to her hometown. She and her widowed daughters-in-law began the journey, but for some reason, Naomi decided it would be better for each of the girls to return to her own mother and wished them well.

Through their ten-year relationship, Naomi had made such a positive impact on them that they both wanted to stay with her and leave their own homeland to go to a foreign land. Naomi insisted, though, that they go back to their mothers. Although deeply saddened, Orpah agreed, but Ruth was apparently more insistent than Naomi and stayed with her, clinging to her. Together, they went to Naomi's hometown in Bethlehem.

Ruth, being a woman of integrity, went out to glean in the fields so that she and Naomi would have a little bit of food. It was customary for workers in fields to harvest the majority of the crops but to not be meticulous with collecting every bit of it. This practice would allow opportunity for poor people to come through the fields and gather up what was left. Ruth found a field and got permission to glean behind the harvesters. The owner of the field was so impacted by her hard work and care for her mother-in-law that when he had the opportunity, he chose to marry her.

Ruth lived visibly with impact. People noticed her integrity, hard work and compassionate spirit.

You and I can live visibly with that kind of impact as we choose to live with integrity and conviction. We have an opportunity to impact others for good with every interaction we have. Embracing the mindset that whenever we're interacting with someone, it's not just that interaction that's influenced. In whatever way we interact with them, they will be able to apply that to their other relationships in the same way. That's part of discipleship.

What opportunities can you identify in your life where you can positively impact others?

20

GET THE HAIR OUT OF YOUR FACE

"'Why do you look at the speck of sawdust in
your brother's eye and pay no attention to the
plank in your own eye?'" –Matthew 7.3

There's a battle for truth! Satan loves lies, but he's seldom blatant about it. He's really good, though, at causing us to see things that are wrong with others, even if those things are not true.

IDENTIFYING AND DEFEATING LIES

Dave and I were standing in the kitchen fairly close to each other. I looked at him as he was putting food in his mouth, and I saw a hair hanging from his hand. Before he took another bite, I had him hold his hand up so I could see to remove the hair. But when he held up his hand, the hair wasn't there. I quickly realized that it was a hair from my own head hanging over my eyes that made it look like it was his issue. As soon as I removed the hair from my own face, I obviously no longer saw one on him.

Not all deceptions are as humorous though. There have been many times when I've felt wounded by someone else only to realize much later that it was something in me that wasn't quite right. Doing our part in making sure we see clearly means willingly clearing out our emotional closets and asking God to search us and reveal those planks in our own eyes.

THE CLOSET IS EMPTY

As long as there are skeletons in our closets, Satan has powerful ammunition to deceive us, and we may even react in harmful ways. When we choose to live with authenticity, being completely open and honest with a trusted friend about what's in us (being willing to look ugly in the presence of love), we can begin to identify and exchange misperceptions for God's truth. We are then better able to maintain peace, joy and love even when there really is a speck in someone else's eye.

Who is a safe person that you can be completely open and honest with? Choose to take a risk and look ugly in the presence of love.

"NOTHING GOOD IS BORN OF LIES."

–Diana Prince, Wonder Woman 1984

WHO & WHAT A WARRIOR FIGHTS FOR

21

THE BATTLE FOR JOY & PEACE

"'Peace I leave with you. My peace I give to
you. I do not give to you as the world gives.
Don't let your heart be troubled or fearful.'"
–John 14.27, CSB

I had a flashback that left me unsettled. A strange allergic reaction sent my son to the ER. As I looked at him, red and swollen with a rash covering his body, I remembered that day about ten years earlier that I had an anaphylactic reaction to a bee sting, and in the current moment, anxiety welled up within me. I knew, mentally, that God was in control and that I had done what I could to help. His situation didn't seem to be life-threatening, and I knew he should be fine. But the "what ifs" started creeping into my thinking. After all, you never know....

I prayed for my son. I prayed for everything I could think of surrounding the situation. And then I kept praying. I realized something about my prayers though. The true purpose of prayer is to release control into the hands of God who is in complete control. I certainly wasn't in control, and that was scary. When I looked at my situation honestly, my prayers were an attempt to maintain control, praying for the specific result that I wanted.

Larry Crabb said this in a conversation he had with God:

> I woke up with my mind focused on a personal concern. Somewhere in the back of my mind, I could sense that I thought You should be doing something about it that You weren't doing. ...I realized...I was trying to fit You into my plans, to use You like I use my car, a vehicle to get me where I want to go. (Crabb, 66 Love Letters)

I've seen how common this is. Instead of praying for God's best and leaving our hands open to receive whatever He has, our tendency might be to pray for the specific result that we want. If it doesn't happen, we can get angry and frustrated with God for not answering our demand. That demand is our attempt to restore joy and peace.

There's a battle for joy and peace. In John 13 and 14, Jesus had just broken the news to His disciples that one of them would betray Him AND that He would physically have to leave them soon, but that He would also come back. He instructed them to care for one another while He was gone, following His example. But it says Jesus' spirit was troubled when He told them that one of them would betray Him. This news was disturbing to all of them.

Jesus experienced a troubled spirit, just like we do, but just as He instructs us, He didn't stay in that troubled place. He felt troubled but then gave it over to God—pouring out His troubled spirit to God. Then He had space for God's sovereign truth to fill Him—the Truth that (to name just a few):

- God's will for Him is better than His own will
- prayer can overpower temptation
- the hope of heaven is greater than the power of the world
- God provides peace of mind and heart whereas the world can, at best, provide occasional peaceful circumstances
- whatever happens that is meant for evil, God can transform for good
- God is madly in love with Him

As His children, God has the same Truth for each of us!

Something that God reminded me of regarding my son was that the battle belongs to Him. I was praying for the resolution I wanted. God reminded me to be careful not to fight as if the battle belongs to me. That will always be my tendency, especially when I feel out of control. When I approach a battle as if it belongs to me, I'm not likely to find

BE CAREFUL NOT TO
FIGHT AS IF THE BATTLE
BELONGS TO YOU

peace. But when I approach it as if it belongs to the Lord, I can rest in knowing the truths on the previous page.

> "'I am leaving you with a gift —peace of mind and heart. And the peace I give isn't like the peace the world gives. So don't be troubled or afraid.'"
> –John 14.27, NLT

In the battle for joy and peace, how are you doing? Look at this list of truths as they relate to you. Write this list in your journal. Read through them as a prayer, thanking God for each one.

- God's will for me is better than my own will
- prayer can overpower temptation
- the hope of heaven is greater than the power of the world
- God provides peace of mind and heart whereas the world can, at best, provide occasional peaceful circumstances
- whatever happens that is meant for evil, God can transform for good
- God is madly in love with me

22

THE BATTLE FOR FREEDOM

"It is for freedom that Christ has set us free. Stand firm, then, and do not let yourselves be burdened again by a yoke of slavery." –Galatians 5.1

There's a battle for freedom! Something that motivates me is to consider if I want to be in the same place ten years from now.

One of the battles we face in securing freedom, ironically, is the battle for surrender. When we avoid surrender, we instead use various coping mechanisms to survive. One of those coping mechanisms is:

I WILL ALWAYS BE _____. Some common answers are: fat, angry, shy, depressed. Statements like this hold us in bondage. These are coping mechanisms because we don't know how to fix them, so we give up and give in to them. They also become cyclical: when we feel fat, our typical response is to be discouraged and do the thing that keeps us fat—overeat. When we're frustrated with an anger problem, we do the thing that grows the problem—we get frustrated and angry. But it's how we've learned to cope. Choosing to give in to our coping mechanisms actually keeps us in control. Staying in control provides an element of comfort, even though it lacks peace.

JUST AS I AM

I looked to others to tell me I was good enough. But good enough for what? I guess, good enough to be acceptable.

Acceptable for what? I think, acceptable for love. I figured if I'm "not good enough," it meant that I wasn't good enough to be loved or accepted... just as I am.

So rather than being "just as I am," and fearing not being accepted, I would try to excel at performance to make sure I was good enough. The problem was, it was no longer "just as I am." There was a high level of performance that I attached to it that didn't allow me the freedom to be "just as I am."

I had to learn to be content with knowing that God accepts me just as I am, replacing my beliefs with His truth. **I'm accepted by Him. I'm completely loved by Him. I don't have to DO anything; my performance is irrelevant.** When I am at peace with that, I am free to be just as I am.

What do you do to cope in life? What would you like to change in your life that feels impossible to change?

Freedom comes from surrendering to the One who knows how to change it even if we don't. It's putting our faith in God's control rather than our own control. With open hands, will you offer to God those things that you can't change?

There is a battle for freedom! In your journal, write the truths that are in bold print above.

"Then you will know the truth, and the truth will set you free." (John 8.32)

23

THE BATTLE FOR COMMUNITY

"The people... came together to seek help
from the Lord...." –2 Chronicles 20.4

The state of our world in recent years has been challenging for everyone, maybe especially in regard to community. We've experienced isolation, mandates, political unrest, violence and tragedy. It's impacted us from our big city streets to our small town schools, in our churches and in our neighborhoods. It's changed the things we do and how we do them. It's messed with our fears and securities. It's messed with our finances and financial outlook. It's messed with our family dynamics and our comfort with simply being in someone else's presence. It's impacted the way we communicate and our demeanor in our communication. It's messed with our sense of community.

I'm an introvert, and one of the ways God has gifted me is with writing. I love to write. I'm comfortable being alone much of the time, and I'm energized by it. But a random thought crossed my mind, and I don't really know how true it is, but the fact that it crossed my mind meant something to me. The thought was this:

I would rather participate in what I am least gifted at than be without meaningful community.

God has wired each of us and gifted us in unique ways, but His first command is to love Him, and second is to love others. We cannot accomplish the second apart from community, and we cannot accomplish the first without the second. That's the dilemma we have faced. We are wired to connect in some sort of community with others by God's design, regardless of our personality tendencies. But life has messed with this. Still, as warrior women in our battle for community, we will press in against the resistance that pushes us out of community. We will recognize our need to stay connected, and we will pursue connection.

FIREPROOF

Within our community, marriage is one of the most fiercely attacked relationships. When the movie, *Fireproof*, was released, Stephen Kendrick (co-writer, co-director and co-producer of the movie) responded in an interview regarding the filming of *Fireproof*:

> Along the way, we found that the enemy knows where to attack based on where God is working. We sought to guard against this by having morning devotions together and prayer times on the set.
>
> When men and women tie the knot, they join their hurts, fears, baggage and imperfections with those of another. They discover how selfish they really are and how sinful their spouse is. The up-close life strips away public facades, exposes us and reveals our fallen

humanity. This can get ugly. At the same time, communication barriers between men and women, work pressures and financial needs usually flare up at some point and add heat to the relationship.

God's Word declares that He is sovereign in the midst of all of this. He created marriage as a beautiful, living, dynamic gift that has His eternal purposes etched in its DNA. Marriage also forces us to grow up and die to ourselves in order to love another imperfect person unconditionally. Marriage can really purify us by fire because it's a picture of Jesus. (*Fireproof*)

Loving another imperfect person unconditionally in community can be challenging. Communication is a big part of the way we love. Certainly not limited to marriage, communication can be quite difficult. We mess up what we write or speak. We mess up what we hear. We're fallible, and communication between people is typically warped to some extent. We need patience with each other to communicate effectively.

One day I was writing something. I intended to write the word gym—you know, as in, "I went to the gym and had a good workout." Well, I didn't realize that I had typed GYN instead of GYM.... It really changes the whole perception and creates confusion.

God never miscommunicates. When something is amiss in our communication with Him, it's because of us. It's our baggage, our stress, fatigue, hunger, loneliness, misunderstanding, frustration, even our excitement and passion. When we humble ourselves, we're better able to hear God effectively. We'll also hear each other more graciously and effectively, and we'll win in the battle for community.

THE VALUE OF A TEAM

Beth Moore described the value of our shield of faith in community. When we stand together with our shields, it becomes a wall—an offensive weapon rather than a defensive weapon—that drives the enemy back. (Moore, shield wall)

I have served with LifeCare Christian Center for 15 years now. I've seen the reality of this concept. As a team, we have joined together in beautiful community, and we have stood together as a line of shields pushing back the darkness. We've witnessed newness of life and brightness in people's lives.

I've had the privilege of working with Larry Crabb's team at a Larger Story event. I recognized the power that was there as I served in community alongside like-hearted people. I saw hope overcome discouragement, community overcome loneliness and realizations overcome impossibilities.

Another ministry I've served with is Life Remodeled where one week each year thousands of people come together to serve and revitalize a community in Detroit. We have witnessed darkness being pushed back as we've stood together, moving forward in faith to make a difference.

What does community look like for you right now?

What has pushed you out of community?

What makes it a battle for you to engage in community?

What steps do you sense would be good to take to grow in community?

24

JUSTICE, MERCY & HUMILITY

(WHAT IS GOOD)

"'"He has shown you, O man, what is good;
And what does the Lord require of you but to
do justly, to love mercy, and to walk humbly
with your God?"' –Micah 6.8, NKJV

He has shown you what is good, has He not? There's something in our conscience, apart from it being seared, that guides us in what is good and right. "They show that the requirements of the law are written on their hearts, their consciences also bearing witness, and their thoughts sometimes accusing them and at other times even defending them." (Romans 2.15)

It's that goodness that God has inherently shown us that helps us in responding with justice, mercy and humility as we move through our lives in agreement with God.

I love superheroes. It's because they, for the most part, encompass Micah 6.8. They have a passion for justice, a sensitivity to the wounds and pain of others, and they lay aside their own desires in order to prioritize care and protection for others. Whether it's Superman, Batman, Wonder Woman or Zorro, each of them encompasses justice, mercy and humility—a dim reflection of the heart of Jesus.

JUSTICE

In Micah 6.8, the Hebrew word for "justly" is mishpah, literally meaning "judgment." Judgment is a tricky subject in our society. We all know someone who tends to judge others apart from love, mercy and righteousness: "*Can you believe what she did?!?*" or "*I can't believe she actually said that!*" or "*What a stupid driver cutting me off like that!*" We know people who judge motives: "*She only said that because she wants something.*" Or "*He treats me that way just to punish me.*" And we all know those who tend to demand that no one judge anyone else: "*Don't judge me; I don't judge you!*" or "*You are so self-righteous!*"

Much of what we call judgment is often either gossip, not understanding a situation, not understanding those who are different from us, or a belief that we are not loved or valued if another perspective is suggested. And those who feel "judged" often feel a sense of disapproval.

So what is judgment, really? And how does it apply to us? There are verses in the Bible that clearly say not to judge but others that guide us in judging. I would encourage you to do your own search on verses about judgment, but for sake of space, I won't tackle all of them here. I do, however, want to address what I believe applies to what and where we battle.

"'Why don't you judge for yourselves what is right?'" (Luke 12.57) The context of this verse is about reconciling differences we have with others. It may include owning up to our own faults/judging ourselves and making amends before someone takes us to an authority to judge. It can also mean humbly allowing ourselves to be wronged, confident that God's justice will ultimately prevail in the end. With this approach, the tables can't be turned on us if the issue is taken to an outside judge. It would be very helpful to seek guidance from a wise friend in situations like this.

"'Stop judging by mere appearances, but instead judge correctly.'" (John 7.24)

"What business is it of mine to judge those outside the church? Are you not to judge those inside? God will judge those outside. 'Expel the wicked person from among you.'" (1 Corinthians 5.12-13)

God is very patient with His children, and there are times when He separates out (or guides us in separating out) someone whose choices are harmful to His other children with the hope that repentance will occur and that person can be welcomed back. It is not at all an issue of judging motives, but rather actions only.

My friends learned that their son had been sexually abusing his sister. Loving both children, my friends knew that they had to remove him from their home in order to protect their daughter. They found a loving place for their son until they could work through all the dynamics including counseling and evidence of repentance. Just because he was removed from where he was doing harm didn't change his parents' love for him. On the contrary, they wanted to see him draw close to God, resolve problematic issues and become successful. It was often painful for everyone, but I watched them walk alongside both of their children, doing their best to love each one unconditionally and help each one unconditionally. They judged well.

The verse in Micah at the beginning of this chapter gives us guidance in how to apply justice or judgment if we read the verse as a whole and not in separate parts. So if God has already shown us what is good, that's our starting point. Judgment must start from a good foundation. Our hearts needs to be enveloped in what God says is good. Along with that, we need to be motivated by kindness and humbly aligning ourselves with God, judging ourselves first according to His righteousness and love.

We don't judge or discern for the purpose of condemning, but rather for:

1. Guarding our hearts / protection for ourselves and others.
2. To draw the person we're "judging" to something better that God has for him or her—not freedom of the world but freedom in Christ. Freedom in Christ sets the heart free and allows the Body of Believers to live together in peace, joy and care for each other.

MERCY

"The steadfast love of the Lord never ceases;
his mercies never come to an end;
(Lamentations 3.22, ESV)

It is humbling and amazing that I can wake up every morning with the confidence that anything bad that I did yesterday (or the day before or the day before that) has been wiped away concerning God's love and kindness toward me. He never gets historical and points out my faults or failures or shortcomings from the past. I get to start over.

I remember heading to college for the first time when I was 18. In my family and childhood community I had developed a reputation for being quiet and shy. I hated those labels and decided that in moving to a college where no one knew me, I had an opportunity to be anything I wanted. I tried to be an outgoing girl on my dorm floor, but it ended up being short lived. First, that's not how God wired me. And second, I had a whole lot of emotional baggage I needed to sort out with God—baggage that had shaped me for many years into the quiet and shy girl that I was.

Ultimately, I didn't have to change the exterior of how I portrayed myself. Instead, God has patiently given me many opportunities over the years to gradually be transformed. Because we have the privilege from God to start over each day, we can also embrace mercy and offer that privilege to others in our battle for others' hearts.

HUMILITY

I love where the apostle Paul says, "My conscience is clear, but that does not make me innocent. ... [The Lord] will bring to light what is hidden in darkness and will expose the motives of the heart." (1 Corinthians 4.4-5) In his desire to align himself with God, he knew that he didn't see himself perfectly. Neither do we. In our approach to others, recognizing our own fallibility is crucial to judging righteously and pouring out mercy and kindness. Another aspect that is crucial is walking with God. Not just to be humble, and not just to walk with Him, but to walk with Him humbly.

I've been a Christian since I was eight years old—nearly 50 years! But all along our spiritual journey, no matter how long we've been on it, we must stay vigilant about being humble and teachable.

Moses was denied entrance into the promised land. He was an amazing, humble spiritual leader, yet he didn't stay vigilant. In Numbers 20.12 God addresses a situation with Moses: "You did not trust in me." One commentary says:

> Moses' leadership faltered in the crucial moment when he stopped trusting God and started acting on his own impulses.
>
> Honoring God in leadership,... we must be careful not to mistake our authority for God's. What can we do to keep ourselves in obedience to God? Meeting regularly with an accountability (or "peer") group, praying daily about the tasks of leadership, keeping a weekly Sabbath to rest in God's presence, and seeking others' perspective on God's guidance are methods some leaders employ. Even so, the task of leading firmly while remaining wholly dependent on God is beyond human capability. If the most humble man on the face of the earth (Num. 12:3) could fail in this way, so can we. (Theology of Work)

As we judge appropriately with mercy from a foundation of goodness, let's stay teachable with a healthy perspective of ourselves, dependent on God's viewpoint and power.

"MY CONSCIENCE IS CLEAR, BUT THAT DOES NOT MAKE ME INNOCENT. ... [THE LORD] WILL BRING TO LIGHT WHAT IS HIDDEN IN DARKNESS AND WILL EXPOSE THE MOTIVES OF THE HEART."

—1 Corinthians 4.4-5

25

THE VOICELESS

"Speak up for those who cannot speak for themselves, for the rights of all who are destitute." –Proverbs 31.8

What does it mean to be a voice for the voiceless? That's the question I asked myself as I read the following verses.

It is not for kings, Lemuel—
 it is not for kings to drink wine,
 not for rulers to crave beer,
 5lest they drink and forget what has been decreed,
 and deprive all the oppressed of their rights. ...
 8Speak up for those who cannot speak for
themselves,
 for the rights of all who are destitute.
 9Speak up and judge fairly;
 defend the rights of the poor and needy.
(Proverbs 31.4-5, 8-9)

These verses encourage him to stay sober-minded so nothing will inhibit his protection of the oppressed, deprived, poor and needy. In these verses, Lemuel's mother is saying not to get lax—not to do anything that would hinder his ability to make sure others are treated right.

If you have a voice, use it for good.

I'm certainly referring to children (born and unborn), the elderly and those with disabilities and limitations, but also lesser thought of situations.

When you're in a work environment where someone is being mistreated and you have a voice with upper management, you can be an advocate for that mistreated person.

When you're doing work for a customer and the company you work for isn't treating the customer right, you can be an advocate for the customer.

When you're a teacher and you notice a very quiet and reserved student, you can speak life into that student and help her find her voice. Being voiceless is oftentimes a result of something that has crushed confidence and caused feelings of insignificance or a lack of value. Being voiceless highlights shame.

I was one of those students. I believed I didn't have a voice. I felt invisible. I felt shame. My swim coach saw me and cared for me. She paid attention to my circumstances and gave me opportunities to grow, thrive and feel valued. She even hired me to do some cleaning at her house to earn money for a USA Swimming membership that I couldn't afford. Her actions toward me helped build my confidence which began to provide framework for restoring my voice.

In my senior year of high school, my English teacher saw me and paid attention to my concerns and fears as well as my interests and strengths. She allowed me to choose the "Word of the Day" at times, allowing my voice to have significance. She invited me to bring my guitar in and, after school, she listened to songs I wrote or learned how to play. Later, she invited me to do a Bible study with her, and she listened to my thoughts.

A family friend saw me and paid attention to my life. She noticed what I was experiencing and choices I was making. She asked me questions about what she saw, drawing me out. She asked about boys I was spending time with, what they were like and what I liked about them. Even though it was unsettling in some ways, I also felt loved and cared for.

A friend and mentor saw me in my weakness, but she also saw what I could be. She took an interest in me, asked questions and gave me opportunities to be heard. She included me in serving alongside her and even playing guitar. Sometime later, she even had me lead worship for an event. She loved me, cared for me and guided me to God's love for me. It grew my confidence and drew me to find more of my voice.

Oftentimes you may not even know what someone is going through. Apart from individuals who spoke life into me and helped restore my voice, my life may have gone in another direction. I think of Cyntoia Brown who, as a teenager, became the victim of sex trafficking, experiencing horrific circumstances. After years of sickening (sometimes there just isn't an adequate word) abuse, she ended up with a life sentence in prison for killing a man who "bought" her. At age 30, however, because of people who learned of her situation and spoke up for her and fought for her, she was released. (Brown)

There are so many who need us. We can battle on their behalf—love them, defend them, speak up for them, empower them—and oftentimes even restore their voice. Their hearts cry out in distress, and God hears them: "Evening, morning and noon I cry out in distress, and he hears my voice." (Psalm 55.17) Maybe He has put you in their path to respond to and battle for their need.

Where do you work? Where do you serve others? Who do you rub shoulders with? Wherever you are, look around to see the needs. Maybe make a list, as God leads, of those you can reach out to. You can make a difference.

"I'M WILLING TO FIGHT FOR THOSE WHO CANNOT FIGHT FOR THEMSELVES."
– Diana Prince, *Wonder Woman 1984*

WHAT A WARRIOR DISCERNS

26

SAMSON WITH A HAIRCUT

"But he said to me, 'My grace is sufficient for you, for my power is made perfect in weakness.'" –2 Corinthians 12.9

Acknowledging weakness can actually make you strong. Especially when you live humbly and peacefully in the midst of your weaknesses, entrusting yourself to God's strength.

Samson was infused with God's strength from birth, but that strength was dependent on never cutting his hair. He did have a couple weaknesses though—ungodly women and vengeance. These weaknesses got him into trouble more than once.

One woman he fell in love with was Delilah, but she was deceitful. She kept betraying him; still, he continued to stay with her. Maybe he felt invincible and that he couldn't be conquered. Ultimately, he gave her the secret of his great strength and she betrayed him with it. As a result, he lost his strength and was taken captive.

We all have strengths, but wisdom tells us to rely on God's strength regardless, recognizing that He is the source of any strength we have. And we all have weaknesses regardless of our strength. If we ever begin to think we're invincible or rely on believing our strengths will outweigh our weaknesses, Satan will be ready to pounce on that opportunity.

When we finally see humility in Samson, he has turned to the Lord for strength, and God gives him a final moment of strength once again. Judges 16.28-30 says,

> [28]Then Samson prayed to the Lord, "Sovereign Lord, remember me. Please, God, strengthen me just once more, and let me with one blow get revenge on the Philistines for my two eyes." [29]Then Samson reached toward the two central pillars on which the temple stood. Bracing himself against them, his right hand on the one and his left hand on the other, [30]Samson said, "Let me die with the Philistines!" Then he pushed with all his might, and down came the temple on the rulers and all the people in it. Thus he killed many more when he died than while he lived.

I wonder what caused Samson to stay with Delilah even though he knew she was deceitful. I wonder why we sometimes return to things that are harmful to us when we know it's not right. Could it be, ironically, a weakness, a fear or maybe unresolved pain? I know that's true for me. Regardless of how strong I become, I know that where the enemy sees even the slightest weakness, he will attack there. It motivates me to stay humbly dependent on God for strength. And even when I stray away and get a bit independent in my thinking, He welcomes me right back when I humbly seek Him again.

A spiritual leader I know has been faithfully married for several decades. He's a devoted and loving husband who delights in his wife. He said once, "I love my wife. I can't imagine ever cheating on her. She's my delight. But I have an enemy who's very deceitful. If he sees an opportunity, he will try to lead me astray, and I have flesh that can be led astray. Given the right circumstances, I could cheat on my wife. Believing that, I don't trust in myself to be faithful; I lean on God to give me strength to be a faithful husband."

In what areas are you strong? Where is your greatest strength? It's quite likely at some point you will be tempted to rely on that strength when temptation comes, or even when something tests or questions your strength. Are you leaning on God in your weakness as well as your strength?

27

DELILAH WITHOUT SCISSORS

> "'The thief comes only to steal and kill and destroy; I came so that they would have life, and have it abundantly.'" –John 10.10, NASB

If Delilah wouldn't have had scissors, she would have found another way to deceive and betray Samson. She was a tool in Satan's hands because her heart wasn't aligned with God's.

Samson was chosen by God, but he had a tendency to be drawn to disreputable women. He united himself with Delilah, but being "unequally yoked" can make us more susceptible to the enemy's destruction. His intention is to kill, steal and destroy—he did that with Samson, and Samson suffered great consequences due to his lack of discernment.

Jesus cautioned his followers to discern what they offer of themselves to others. "'Do not give dogs what is sacred; do not throw your pearls to pigs. If you do, they may trample them under their feet, and turn and tear you to pieces." (Matthew 7.6) In Jesus' time, dogs were typically considered working animals to hunt and shepherd. They did not carry high value, and to call someone a dog was a derogatory statement alluding to them being evil. So Jesus cautioned not to give dogs what is sacred—don't give away what God has grown in you and gifted you with to someone who won't value it. The same with throwing pearls to pigs—pigs were considered unclean and destructive and were rejected as an offering. So it makes sense that we shouldn't give our valuable skills, gifts and blessings to pigs—they will trample them and not value them. So what do we do?

For some reason, Samson kept giving in to Delilah's pleas for information, at first as if it was a game, but ultimately giving her what was sacred. What is sacred to you? Oftentimes, we want to keep giving people compassion, grace and understanding. There's certainly a time for that, but if grace is requested incessantly, and tolerance is requested over and over, it may be time to speak the truth in love. Guide that person into responsible and godly behavior with their character. Discerning circumstances of course, it could mean saying, "Whenever we go together to that event, you drink too much and disrespect me. If that behavior continues, I will not be going with you any longer to that event." It helps the other person and grows their character when you call them to be who God designed them to be—men and women clothed in the fruit of the spirit. And that will bring glory to God.

When we don't discern boundaries like this, it gives the enemy an opportunity to get in and kill, steal and destroy the valuable things God has given. (John 10.10) Just like he was able to destroy Samson through his lack of discernment with Delilah, he can also bring destruction on us when we make unwise choices. Be a discerning warrior.

Do you have a situation that might require boundaries?

WHAT A WARRIOR

FIGHTS AGAINST

28

THE OPPOSITE OF LOVE

"Above all, maintain constant love for one
another, since love covers a multitude of sins."
–1 Peter 4.8, CSB

People use all kinds of excuses to explain why they can't get along. But the thing is, they are just excuses. My first big conflict with my husband after we were married didn't have anything to do with a major problem. It had to do with taking the trash out. Looking back thirty years, I'm just shaking my head about it; but back then, a major conflict was happening. The reality was that it had nothing to do with trash and everything to do with believing I wasn't loved, valued and heard. Something about that trash situation tapped into my insecurities, and I lashed out, believing he was the enemy.

Unity can be very challenging, especially in our marriages. That makes sense though—it's the relationship that God chose to illustrate His relationship with the Trinity—relationship as it should be. So marriage, of course, will be one of Satan's primary targets of attack. Still, he will attack any relationship where he can get a foothold.

As we talked about in the last chapter, Satan has come to kill, steal and destroy. What does he want to kill, steal and destroy? I believe it's love. He is opposed to God. God IS love, and God's greatest command is to love Him and to love others. And it's love that covers sin. So Satan will certainly be opposed to our intentions to love. Whether it's in a marriage, with our kids, with our parents or our siblings, with our close community and friends, He will do everything he can to divide us. He will try to convince us of how we don't belong together and how division, finding faults and being alone will be better. He will be really good at convincing us that the trash is the problem in our relationship. But if he can't convince us of that, he'll likely convince us that it's the other person that's the problem rather than seeing the reality of the spiritual battle going on behind the scenes.

In the trash situation, I couldn't see at that point that the enemy was having a field day with me, keeping me distracted with trying to manage my fears by trying to *make* my husband value me in a specific way. I didn't recognize that God wanted to use the situation to refine me. My husband was one of the tools He was choosing to use. I believed I wouldn't be loved if my husband didn't value me in a specific way. Once I began a healing journey to see God's perspective in my beliefs, I could finally begin moving beyond responding in fear to responding in love.

Journal about this. Have you had a conflict with someone over something trivial? What did the situation trigger in you? When you begin to ask God about His perspective in what's triggering you, you'll be able to begin moving beyond the pain or discomfort you feel in those interactions.

PEOPLE PLEASING OR CONFLICT AVOIDANCE

I studied people. I studied them for the purpose of pleasing them—or more accurately, keeping them happy with me, keeping them from being upset.

Why?

Because when they were upset, it scared me to the point where I struggled with IBS for many years (sorry if that's TMI). People being upset or angry tapped into some deep memories and intense emotion. It felt so unsafe that in order to survive, I believed I had to do everything in my power to keep them from being upset, especially with me.

The way it played out was that I stayed keenly aware of what upset people and did my best to avoid those things. One time a couple friends were at my house. They began to argue about something, and kept arguing. I was very uncomfortable, and actually felt a bit panicky. I tried to interject some comments here and there to help them resolve their conflict. It was really more self-serving though, attempting to make my environment more peaceful because I was uncomfortable. Then I heard God speaking to me about the situation: "It's okay for them to be a mess." I realized that they needed to wrestle through this in order to successfully get to the other side of it. In my own discomfort, I was trying to clean up a mess that was actually serving a purpose in refining each of them. It was a good lesson for me in resting in God's peace in my own heart while I allow others to wrestle in order to get to a place of peace in their own hearts.

ALIGNMENT

As I mentioned before, I love superhero movies, especially Wonder Woman. What is it that draws me though?

I don't have a desire to "rebuild the Multiverse." I do connect with her heart though. But there's something more. I noticed that she's not restrained by fear. She's empowered and free to live out her passion and calling. I want to see God's transformation in my life in such a way that I can freely live out who He has called me to be and bravely pursue all that He's called me to do. I can't do it just by willpower though. Romans 12.2 says to "be transformed by the renewing of your mind." How does God transform people's minds? With truth. Not a skewed idea of "*my truth*" or "*your truth*" that is popular in our culture. That thinking provides a sense of affirmation but really isn't helpful. Instead, transformation like Romans 12.2 talks about will happen when we get God's truth in place of the beliefs we hold that are not aligned with Him. It's discovering where we're not aligned with God's thinking and truth. Our unwanted emotions, like fear, can be helpful in discovering some of our unaligned thinking that keeps us from freely living out who He created us to be. (As a side note, if you're interested, LifeCare Christian Center can provide guidance in walking you through this process, both in person and virtually—contact info is in the back of this book.)

"THEY WIN BY MAKING YOU THINK YOU'RE ALONE."

–Zori to Po on Kajimi (*Star Wars: Episode IX*)

29

FATIGUE

"'I, Daniel, was worn out. I lay exhausted for several days. Then I got up and went about the king's business.'" –Daniel 8.27

What keeps me from being a warrior?

I'm tired.

I'm comfortable right where I am.

My joints ache, my back hurts, something weird is going on with my car and I'm hungry. I have to catch up on finances, I have to prepare for a meeting tomorrow and I have to do my reading for my Bible study.

Sometimes I can be wimpy and finicky. I live in Michigan. Two months out of the year I'm too hot. Eight months out of the year I'm too cold.

Other times I really am weary—fighting battles that are exhausting. That's when it's time for me to drop my sword and let God refresh me. He does that, ya know?

This world is tiring, and we do get tired. But our arms need to be strong. We can't walk around carrying a sword with a limp arm. We need to wield the sword with strength and intention.

What's stirring in your weariness?

Having a weekly Sabbath rest is crucial. And sometimes we need extra rest. Returning to our First Love and resting with Him can be so refreshing. I mentioned before that I love this version of Matthew 11.28:

"'Come to Me, all you who labor and are heavy-laden and overburdened, and I will cause you to rest. [I will ease and relieve and refresh your souls.]'" (AMPC)

Daniel had an experience with God that completely wore him out. God gave him the opportunity to rest afterward, and when he was ready, he returned to the work God had for him. Remembering to use the opportunities God gives us to rest allows us to be our best for Him.

There are other times when we feel worn out because of mistreatment. The Israelites ended up in Egypt so they could be saved from a famine, thanks to Joseph's faithfulness (and of course, God's sovereignty). They were there for several generations and filled the land. A new king came to power and was afraid. His fear was that the Israelites were so numerous and powerful that they might fight against the Egyptians and defeat them. (Exodus 1.9-11) Rather than building unity with them, the new king decided that he should be controlling by making them slaves and wearing them down.

Do you see ways that our enemy wears us down? I see it in political issues, social issues, health issues, etc. And he convinces us to wear ourselves down (working excessively, being in or having our kids in numerous activities, and doing many things to an extreme). Our intentions are good, but we end up not being our best, and then, like the Israelites, we become slaves—worn out and trapped. When you sense those feelings of being worn out and trapped, take notice and ask God about it. Maybe it's just a challenging season, or maybe there's a change He would have you make.

WORN OUT TO GIVING UP

My husband and I decided to buy a house that would be more conducive to ministry we wanted to do. God provided, led and blessed in the whole process. From the beginning, we could see God doing amazing and beautiful things.

Satan is not real keen on such a thing. After about a year in our new house, I looked back and realized why I felt like I had been walking through a battlefield like Wonder Woman deliberately walking across "no man's land." The enemy launched heavy fire on her, but she still moved forward, ducking behind her shield as it took the heavy gunfire. As she did this, the allies were able to descend on the enemy.

Through that first year in our new house, as I held up my shield of faith, my attention had been turned to the heavy fire of:

- the refrigerator breaking down
- the garage door light acting possessed as it would flash on and off non-stop
- invisible spiders attacking me outside leaving me with over a hundred bites in two months
- frog invasion in my koi pond
- the pool company neglecting to remove two plugs so the chlorine wouldn't circulate
- chimney repair needed
- electrical problems
- unpredictable smoke detectors
- multiple service providers being unsatisfactory
- weed invasion problems
- rabbit & chipmunk invasion problems
- loose knobs
- loose light fixtures
- squeaky doors
- garbage disposal problems
- furnace humidifier problems
- multiple power outages
- and a big zoo problem in our attic
- ...just to name a few

We also had general maintenance beyond what we were accustomed to. And we had been trying to set up our house to make it conducive to hosting retreats. It was tiring, but a battle worth fighting. These are things that will bounce off my shield as I trust in the Lord's faithfulness, and in the process, loving God and loving people will prevail.

As I spent some time with God, I heard His words to me:

> My love,
>
> I created you to live in My bright light. I know you are drawn to the light. I know you get sucked into and dragged down by the dark places. I know...and I still love you, but I long for you to dwell constantly in the beauty, safety, peace and joy of My presence. When you, over and over, throughout each day, remember Me, who I am, who I've made you to be, and all the things I've done, you will be able to not only dwell in My bright light—you will also radiate My light. This will light up the world around you.
>
> Hold onto Me as I hold onto you.
>
> –your Best Love

BE STILL

My whole body was fatigued and sore. I had spent four straight days pushing myself with exercise. The fifth day was a day of rest—physically and spiritually. I spent time with God sitting on my deck, talking to Him about what I needed and thanking Him for all that He'd done (Philippians 4.6-7). I connected with Him (my Life Source) through His Word, music, sharing my heart and listening to His heart. Just as He said to the stormy sea, and it became still, He also spoke to my heart, with His ability to tame its chaos, "Peace, be still."

What is He speaking to your heart right now as you share your heart with Him?

30

GIANTS OR SQUIRRELS

"Today the LORD will conquer you"
–1 Samuel 17.46a, NLT

If we don't see it in our immediate vicinity, all we have to do is look at the news to know there's a war going on that starts in the spiritual realm and invades the hearts of people. Today alone the news is telling me of:

- postal service official accused of taking bribes for government contracts
- police car struck in hit-and-run
- a boy murdered by his mom's boyfriend and stashed in a freezer
- hostile work environment leads to resignation
- religious persecution in China
- Russia attacking Ukraine
- school shooting perpetrator admired Hitler
- three convicted in $18 million Covid relief scam
- woman reporting sexual assault in Qatar faces jail and 100 lashes
- two men robbed store at gunpoint

- man steals retired police officer's car at gunpoint
- drug trafficking
- labor trafficking
- sexual assault
- sex trafficking
- impending cyberattacks

That's just today, and really that's just the tip of the iceberg.

Evil giants surround us in this world. They are tools in the enemy's hands. If our focus stays on the giants, it can feel daunting and hopeless. It feels like giants will conquer us, but not all giants are big. Some are huge, but some are not.

The little giant that surrounded me recently and felt like it would conquer me was a squirrel. It was actually in my presence for a few months. It was in October when I occasionally noticed a squirrel climbing the brick on my house. I didn't think much of it at first. Eventually, I started noticing that squirrel had something in its mouth—a nut. Intriguing, but I still didn't think much of it. It wasn't until I started hearing what sounded like scratching on the roof above my bedroom (that also contains my office/writing space) that I started to really take notice. It was December by this time, and I set a live trap, but it wasn't interested in the peanut butter that froze quickly.

We decided to climb up into the attic opening and realized that the attic was covered with blown in insulation—not conducive for novices to walk over, and the layout of the attic didn't allow for a visual inspection. So we were stuck waiting for someone who could help. While waiting, that squirrel clearly moved into the attic without paying rent and apparently set up a wood shop—what sounded like sawing planks, moving loads of lumber and building something massive—possibly even rewiring our house. I was distracted by him—convinced that at some point he would either carve his way into my bedroom or chew through wiring in the attic that would cause our electricity to go out. I know they can be really destructive. I just didn't want to find out how destructive.

A squirrel or anything that impersonates a giant can be distracting and intimidating. I wanted to ignore it, but I had to deal with it. I also needed to ignore it at times in order to follow my calling (including focusing to write). Discernment of my battle was key.

The boy, David, discerned when to run into the battle to face the giant, Goliath. God stirred something in him that wouldn't allow him to turn away. He had conviction about what was right, and he didn't entertain fear, distraction or intimidation. The rest of the army was fearful and stayed hidden from the giant. They tried to ignore the giant, probably hoping he would just go away.

What happens when you hide from a giant? He seldom goes away. Instead, he taunts the righteous even more. And then bitterness has fertile ground to grow in you. Bitterness destroys people more than the unrighteous acts of a giant.

What are the giants you're facing today?

One of the ways David fought various battles was in encouraging himself. Of the many battles David faced, he endured intense attacks on his life by a man he should have been able to trust. There were also attacks on his family when they were kidnapped. 1 Samuel 30:6 says David encouraged himself in the Lord. He looked to God in his distress. Psalm 7 is a song he sang to the Lord in his distress: "I come to you for protection, O Lord my God. Save me from my persecutors—

rescue me!" (Psalm 7.1, NLT) Not only does singing in worship encourage us and give us strength and peace, but it is also the very thing that defeats the real enemy, Satan, because he cannot stand to be in the presence of God being praised. David looked to God in his distress, but he also ended his psalms with trusting and aligning with God even before he knew what the outcome would be.

My husband and I were able to enter our squirrel battlefield by getting someone to come inspect our attic. We found that we had an invasion of squirrels, mice and bats (that were all evicted in five days)!! But until the eviction happened, I had to choose to not let my giant-impersonating squirrel (or zoo) determine my level of joy and peace, and certainly not determine a state of bitterness in me. As I praised God for His sovereignty in my situation, confident in His plan to slay the giant that taunted me, I could peacefully write. I was able to fulfill my calling, despite the attempted distraction of my enemy, knowing that my God is the Great Giant Slayer.

"Stay alert! Watch out"
(1 Peter 5.8, NLT)

INVISIBLE GIANTS

One thing I've learned is that where God is working, the enemy is not far behind. 1 Peter 5.8-9a (NLT) says, "Stay alert! Watch out for your great enemy, the devil. He prowls around like a roaring lion, looking for someone to devour. Stand firm against him, and be strong in your faith."

He opposes the great work that God is doing in, through and around us—those of us who are seeking to follow Him. WE are who Satan is looking to devour. He will pay attention to our weaknesses, and he will watch and wait for us to be at a low point (maybe hungry, angry, lonely, tired, fearful, hormonal, injured, compromised, in need, ...). At an opportune time, he will attack—maybe with temptation toward a false sense of fulfillment, relief or security.

I had been agitated for a few days, but I had forgotten about Satan's shrewd presence prowling around waiting to pounce. God was working in our lives in some profound ways. He had poured out blessing on us, setting us up for more amazing ministry opportunities—big things He wanted to accomplish as He used us. And the enemy hated it. Ephesians 6.12 says we are not fighting against flesh and blood but against an enemy we can't readily see—in the spiritual realm.

It reminds me that my parent, my spouse, my child, my friend or my neighbor—they are not my enemy, but Satan wants me to think they are. So as Ephesians 6 goes on to say, we need to put on spiritual armor to stand against him, not giving him any opportunity. It means believing the best about the flesh and blood people in our midst. It means running from anything that could cause temptation toward sin. It means watching carefully for red flags. It means staying involved in community—maybe even choosing to be

"'I WOULD HAVE DESPAIRED UNLESS I HAD BELIEVED THAT I WOULD SEE THE GOODNESS OF THE LORD IN THE LAND OF THE LIVING.'"
-Psalm 27.13, NASB1995

"completely" open with another wise person who can be a mentor (which I chose to start doing more than a decade ago). It means leaning into God's strength when we're weak AND when we think we're strong. You may want to identify more of what it means for you specifically to not give Satan an opportunity.

My agitation had been because I forgot who my real enemy was, and I started looking at what others were doing or not doing and letting my attitude be triggered by my disappointments. While God is working in our midst to bring LIFE, Satan is stepping up to oppose His work and attempt to cause us to fall. He wants to destroy integrity and life, to steal our joy and peace, to kill unity and relationship, but he'll deceive us with what initially looks tempting.

There is a beautiful thing about leaning into God as we battle the giants: all of those giants can allow God's power to be put on display.

What giants are you facing that will allow God's power to be put on display?

GOLIATH:
THE GIANT THAT
ALLOWED GOD'S POWER
TO BE PUT ON DISPLAY.

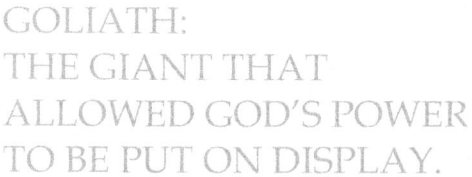

31

A SUPERHERO VS. GOD

"...you have struggled with God and with humans
and have overcome." –Genesis 32.28b

A superhero vs. God is not about them battling each other. It's about a battle within our hearts. Maybe we'd rather have a superhero than God because of what we see on the surface.

One difference between superheroes and God is that superheroes try to stop evil; they attempt to stand in the way of evil. Of course, they can only be in one place at any given time, so we see a superhero's limitations in that sense. God being spirit can be everywhere all at once, so He's able to work everywhere at the same time.

Unlike the superhero who works in the realm of what we see, most of God's battles, including on our behalf, are in the spiritual realm. The spiritual realm is an even more powerful aspect of reality that we are unable to see as we are. Since God gives people free will, He won't stand in the way of free choice unless He's unable to use it for good for His children. For me, and you if you love Him, everything that touches our lives is molded for good (Romans 8.28).

On the surface, it looks like superheroes work hard to defeat evil. They may even be disheartened by their limitation of only being able to be in one place at one time. On the other hand, it could look like God is just standing back doing nothing even though He could be working everywhere all at once. But on the contrary, a superhero is only able to work on the surface, whereas God is able to work in many dimensions.

I can relate to the superhero who wants to eradicate pain and suffering. It's harder to understand God who allows pain and suffering within His magnificent plan and purpose. But like the superhero, I only see the physical world around me, mostly unaware of the deeper battles that God is fighting.

I think of Daniel who battled on behalf of his people. He prayed for God's help, and then three weeks went by before an angel showed up to let him know that God had heard him when he first prayed. The delayed response was because the angels had been fighting a battle in the spiritual realm on Daniel's behalf for 21 days. I'm not even sure what that means really. It's mind boggling. Since God is all powerful, he could defeat an enemy immediately. But that battle lasted 21 days. What was that about? Or is it a battle related to someone's heart? Daniel's heart? His people's hearts?

Look at Jacob. He physically wrestled with a physical manifestation of God. Again, God's vast power could have easily defeated Jacob, but that wasn't His purpose. It seems His purpose was to allow Jacob to wrestle with Him until there was a change—in his heart, his mind, his spirit.

Superheroes seek to change the physical world—things that only impact this life. God does concern Himself with the physical world, but more importantly, He is out to change hearts, minds and spirits—things that will last forever. The intense battles He's fighting are beyond our vision.

WHEN A WARRIOR IS CALLED TO THE BATTLEGROUND

32

MARCHING ORDERS

"Praise be to the Lord my Rock,
who trains my hands for war,
my fingers for battle.
²He is my loving God and my fortress,
my stronghold and my deliverer,
my shield, in whom I take refuge,
who subdues peoples under me."
–Psalm 144.1-2

My friend was in the Navy Reserves. Being in the Reserves, she never really thought she'd be deployed to full time active duty overseas. But with her husband and two young children at home, she was called to battle halfway around the world. Her heart was shattered at having to leave her family. She would miss her son's second birthday. She would miss the connection with her kids with driving them to school. She would miss daily interaction with her husband. Everything that was familiar was uprooted. The language would be different. Daily routines would be different. Where she slept, what she ate, what she did in her free time—it would all be different.

She always knew this was a possibility. But it became a reality. She chose this path because she believed in her country, in protecting the people of her country, in providing hope for her children, and her children's children. She signed up knowing that she would be trained to go to the battleground. And she was trained. She was equipped and prepared.

When the time came to be deployed, she questioned her readiness. Was she adequately equipped? Could she do what she was being called to do?

I wrestle with those same questions when God calls me into the various battlegrounds He has for me, personally. I imagine we all wrestle to some extent with those questions.

As you finish this book about being equipped as a Warrior Woman, maybe you're uncertain about your readiness to enter battlegrounds. Maybe you question if you're adequately equipped. Can you really do what God calls you to do?

God has prepared you for such a time as this. Fortunately, the only thing you need to be is WILLING. My friend chose to be willing to go to the battlefield, trusting that she had been adequately equipped for her calling. Her skills were desperately needed, and she trusted those who called her to action.

You, too, are essential. You are living in a time when you are desperately needed. Will you trust the One who calls you to action? The One who will equip you, empower you, and in the process, enjoy you as well?

You are called to the battleground, Warrior Woman!

WARRIOR WOMAN: BATTLEGROUND
due out summer 2023

AFTERWORD

We are all called to be Warriors for Christ as Kelly so eloquently challenged us to be. We may be warring in our prayer closets or warring out in the front lines of the battle. On the front lines, it may be through our acts of service, warring for the drug addict or alcoholic, the homeless, the unborn, the lost, the broken, the unhealthy, ...

We are all called to participate in the battle in some way to fight for and minister to "the least of these." Maybe you have been in that season or are possibly in that season right now, as Jesus described in the gospels. If you have been on the sidelines, what Kelly has written will help you to become willing to link arms with others and join the spiritual army for the cause of Christ! We need you!

I'd encourage every one of you to take time to go back and look at your responses to Kelly's questions throughout this book, and consider what you wrote in your journal, allowing each page to penetrate your heart and mind completely so it affects your life going forward.

Kelly Hawkins has prepared the way for all of us. Whether you are just beginning boot camp, in the middle of it or completing that leg of your journey, you need to know and be reminded, as she reminded each of us, God is on our side, and He wants to use us in mighty ways!

War on Warrior Women!

Lillian Easterly-Smith

WHAT IS LIFECARE?

LifeCare Christian Center is a nonprofit, interdenominational organization in the service of providing individuals and families in the community with physical, spiritual, emotional and relational support while walking through life's challenges. We all have gone through life crises or at least know someone who has. LifeCare is for those who have a desire to overcome issues of the heart, learn life skills, and have a longing to change. At LifeCare, they find restoration, peace and purpose.

Founded by Lillian Easterly-Smith, LifeCare Christian Center provides a fresh and innovative approach to personal growth and healing by giving care and support to individuals and families within the community. LifeCare's mission is to offer opportunities for life transformation, and we strive to achieve this objective by providing a safe place of ongoing care and support for people of all ages from trained individuals who have been through similar life circumstances.

Lillian, herself, is an accomplished teacher, speaker and leader in the fields of Christian care, recovery and support group ministry with more than two decades of experience.

LifeCare offers various opportunities for growth and healing. Below is a list of many of those opportunities:

- **Group Care** (care, support, recovery) A detailed list can be found on our website.
- **Life Enrichment Opportunities** (workshops, seminars, classes, retreats)
  Anger, Stress, Abuse, Health & Wellness, Marriage Skills, Finances, Substance Abuse, Spiritual Growth
- **"The Great Exchange" – Experiential Healing Weekends** for Women

These weekends help women recognize who they are in Christ and experience healing, growth and truth that is life transforming. It's a safe place to be real and experience God.

- **Pastoral/ Chaplaincy Care** - Funerals, Weddings, Crisis Care, etc.
- **Life Coaching**
  Setting goals, planning & accountability accomplish results. Areas of focus are: career, education, relational, spiritual growth and many other life issues. See possibilities! Set Priorities! Find the confidence to fulfill God's purpose for life!
- **Transformation Prayer Ministry**
  Opportunities for focused prayer to expose lies that cause painful emotions, allowing those lies to be replaced with truth.
- **Leadership Training & Development of Care & Support Ministries for Churches and Para-Church Organizations**
- **Professional Counseling**
  Searching for a competent, professional counselor with the same values as you? Our contracted professionals as well as those on our referral list have been screened and interviewed to be sure you will be receiving care and competent counseling from someone you can trust.
- **Professional Interventions** (addictions & compulsive behaviors)
  Based on the "Love First" approach.
- **Living Well** - Classes and seminars for nutrition, exercise, and how to develop a healthy lifestyle.

Groups and life enrichment opportunities are offered periodically during the year. A full listing is available at www.lifecarechristiancenter.org.

LifeCare is a non-profit 501(c)3 organization and solely operates from charitable donations that are tax deductible.

ACKNOWLEDGMENTS

I am thankful for so many who have impacted my life in beautiful ways over the years. There are a few that I would especially like to highlight as they have influenced me greatly in being a warrior for Jesus and supported this leg of the journey.

Lillian Easterly-Smith—for helping me to learn how to put on many pieces of my armor, and for protecting my heart with tenderness when I lose my grip on my shield.

Candi Beemer—for helping to sharpen my sword and tighten my belt of truth through your faithful friendship filled with discernment, guidance and beautiful care for my heart.

Rachael Crabb—for sharing your heart and wanting to hear mine. You help me tie my shoes of peace that keep me running.

Marilyn Osborne—for delighting in my helmet of salvation with your life-giving words to me, for savoring the written words that God gives me, and for sharing them with so many others.

Diana Pintar—for recognizing when a weight has been placed on me, and stepping in with strength and grace to lift it off. And then seeking to make sure my armor is secure. Also for your wisdom and editorial guidance to enhance these pages.

My Bible In A Year and Together With The Word sisters—for helping to empower me to use my sword effectively.

Renee Allen—for the times you provided a safe place to repair my shield, sharpen my sword, adjust my helmet and retie my shoes.

Cheryl Rosten—for believing I had a mission, knowing God would use me and trusting He would show me how.

My LifeCare/GEW team—for standing firm alongside me to guide others in putting on their armor. I love that we stand in community together with our shields to push back darkness.

Donna Haught and Lora Gray—for conversations that matter and empower me. For our community.

Kep Crabb, Kris Gamble & the whole Larger Story team—for the privilege of joining in the battle alongside you—like-minded and like-hearted warriors.

Dave—for believing I have something worth sharing and empowering me to do just that. For conversations that inspire my thoughts. For loving me just as I am, and for helping me find my shoes of peace when I lose them.

For many who've walked alongside me in various ways—my armor is better secured because of you.

And certainly, I'm thankful for all those (and there are many of you) who cheered me on and longed to read this book (friends, family, fellow authors, ministry leaders, my chiropractor)—you have strengthened me more than you'll ever know.

It may sound cliché, but I'm beyond thankful to God for giving me purpose and hope, for walking and fighting alongside me (or ahead of me to prepare the way), for being patient with me, loving me beyond comprehension, delighting in me, for wanting me, for reviving my computer when it just stopped, for having a battle plan that includes me and empowers me, for giving me armor that fits, for giving me an army to fight alongside me, ...

REFERENCES

Brown, Cyntoia. 2019. https://www.cbsnews.com/amp/news/cyntoia-
   brown-to-be-released-from-prison-after-killing-man-as-teen-
   sex-trafficking-victim-2019-08-06/

Coyle, Neva. *A Woman of Strength: Reclaim Your Past, Seize Your
   Present, and Secure Your Future.* Servant, 1997.

Crabb, Larry. *66 Love Letters.* Nashville: Thomas Nelson, 2009.

Crabb, Larry. *The Papa Prayer.* Nashville: Thomas Nelson, 2007.

Dickens, Charles. *Great Expectations.* Oxford University Press, 1998
   (first published Jan. 1, 1860).
   https://www.goodreads.com/work/quotes/2612809-great-
   expectations

Fireproof. Kendrick Brothers Films, 2008.
   https://baptistnews.com/article/directorwriterrecountsmaki
   ngoffireproof/#.YfB-Xv7MJPY

For King & Country. Written by Joel David Smallbone, Benjamin
   Glover, Luke James Smallbone, Tedd T. "Shoulders". *Run
   Wild, Live Free, Love Strong*: 2014.

Foundations.
   https://www.foundationsforfreedom.net/Topics/Grace/Grac
   e013.html

Moore, Beth. Instagram. 2020.
   https://www.instagram.com/p/B9M_UennwPh/

Moore, Beth. "Over Our Heads". 2008.
   https://blog.lproof.org/2008/12/over-our-heads.html

Moore, Beth. *Praying God's Word Day by Day.* B&H Books, 2006, Aug
   15 (Psalm 18).

Moore, Beth. "Shield of Faith". 2021.
   https://www.youtube.com/watch?v=5TGX9dRSQlg

Paris, Twila. "The Warrior is a Child". *Signature Songs.* Greentree,
   1984.

Star Wars: Episode IX – The Rise of Skywalker. 2019.

Theology of Work. "Moses' Unfaithfulness at Meribah".
https://www.theologyofwork.org/old-testament/numbers-and-work/moses-unfaithfulness-at-meribah-numbers-202-13

Todaysmilitary.com. "Boot Camp".
https://www.todaysmilitary.com/joining-eligibility/boot-camp

Wickham, Phil. Written by Brian Johnson (Bethel). "Battle Belongs". *Hymn of Heaven*, 2020.

Wonder Woman. 2017.
https://www.imdb.com/title/tt0451279/?ref_=fn_al_tt_1

Wonder Woman: 1984. 2020.
https://www.imdb.com/title/tt7126948/?ref_=fn_al_tt_1

Made in the USA
Monee, IL
03 January 2025

73111128R00095